UNTOUCHED BY TIME

UNTOUCHED BY TIME

A Biography of an Andalusian Village

Albert Rowe

The Book Guild Ltd
Sussex, England

The Book Guild Ltd
25 High Street,
Lewes, Sussex

First published 1998
© Albert Rowe, 1998

Set in Times by
Rowland Phototypesetting Ltd
Bury St Edmunds, Suffolk

Printed in Great Britain by
Antony Rowe Ltd
Chippenham, Wiltshire

A catalogue record for this book is
available from the British Library

ISBN 1 85776 371 8

In loving memory of Joan; and for our family

Sunt lacrimae rerum et mentem mortalia tangunt.
[There are tears shed for things and being mortal touches
  our heart.]

Virgil, Aeneid, I, 461.

PROLOGUE

We went, my wife and I, to live in this Andalusian village soon after Generalísimo Federico Franco died on 20 November 1975.

We found the village quite untouched by time. The villagers were living as they had always lived, following in the footsteps of their forefathers, happy and content with their isolation. They had no TV (that all-powerful instigator of change), no radio, no newspapers, no phones. The affairs of the world outside neither interested nor concerned them.

There was not a square metre of plastic to be seen. They grew their crops in the open fields, the *vega*. They dunged their plots with pig, goat, chicken and rabbit manure. Occasionally they bought loads of cow dung; there were no cows here, pasture was too scarce, the summer heat too intense. Their plough, handed down from father to son, often so worn it had to be kept together with rope lashings, was pulled by a pair of docile and hardworking mules, as it had always been. Their only tool was the *asada*, a big spade-shaped hoe, which served as spade, hoe, rake and drill for sowing seeds and planting out seedlings.

It was not many years before change came; gradually at first, then with increasing speed. How fortunate we had been, though, Joan and I, living there during those few magical years when the whole way of life – values, customs, thinking, language – was as it had always been, preserved as it were in amber.

The series of incidents described are all true, the numerous vignettes drawn from life. I have not attempted a strict chronology: my aim has been to give a picture of life in the village as it unfolded in front of us, a life of which we soon became a part.

vii

1

The morning after the house was finished and the furniture in place, the women and their pre-school children of our *barrio*, our part of the village, knocked at the door. They stood there smiling. Said nothing, knowing we knew what was expected.

We smiled also. Nodded. 'Hullo. Good morning. Come in, come in. Pleased to see you.'

They shuffled in – there must have been about 20 all told – still silent, still smiling. Stopped in amazement at the sight of the long living room, formerly three rooms. And the kitchen – the kitchen only separated from the other room by a waist-high wall with a marble counter on top. Pretty marble, though.

We saw how puzzled they were. All the rooms in their houses were small, even though their families were big. What, then, did our neighbours here, only two of them, want with such space? Who knows how the minds of *los ingleses* (pronounced in their dialect *lawingléh*) worked? Well, each person had the right to their own opinion; a saying they had adopted only after the death of Generalísimo Franco.

And the walls. Still limed and as rough as they were before, the back wall still the solid rock of the hillside, still as ugly as ever. The heavy old door they had just entered, still with the ancient massive lock and key, the *rejas*, bars, that guarded the windows, the wooden shutters themselves, all the same as before. Draughts would still blow in through the cracks when the winter winds beat against the front of the house. Not to mention that wind from the Sahara, laden with yellow dust. Well, if this was how *lawingléh* wished to live . . .

Of course *lawingléh* had told everybody they wanted to keep the village house they had bought looking exactly as it had always looked. Thank goodness, though, they now had *azulejos*, such pretty tiles, on the floor, so much better than the previous concrete. The ceiling, too, was now smoothly plastered, the old exposed reeds gone.

Over these reeds, a layer of earth, stones and concrete had served as roof – a flat roof that leaked badly when it rained, which thank heaven was very seldom. The new roof, the *terraza*, was now strong enough to be on. That they knew because they had seen *lawingléh* and the workmen on it.

The children were by now grouped around the three dyed-blue sheepskin rugs we had bought in Skipton market. What were these strange objects for? They were like nothing they had ever seen. They knelt down, ran their hands over the thick soft wool. So lovely to touch, they brushed their cheeks to and fro over them.

The mothers summoned the children to their side. My wife led the way up the solid rock steps with their taxingly high treads to the bedrooms, the visitors carefully avoiding stepping on the rugs.

At the top, the leading woman stopped. Was this lustrous blue thing covering the floor a carpet? Dare she walk on it? Were not carpets things the rich hung on their walls?

'*Pase, pase, por favor*,' Joan had to say to each woman in turn. Each murmured her surprised admiration, the children again kneeling to smooth their cheeks over the pile.

And the twin beds. No matrimonial bed here. Hmm . . .

Their disapproval was almost tangible. What a contrast to one of their husbands when he saw them. He looked at Joan, his eyes shining. '*¡Qué idea buenisima!*' His hands darted to and fro, crossing one another. 'What caprice! Sometimes the woman crosses over, sometimes the man, it all depends. What caprice. What a splendid idea!'

We processed through the back door of the second bedroom and out onto the *terraza*. The women gathered in a group. They approved of its size, the brown tiles that covered it, the view of the cultivated *vega* that stretched away below, the hills that ringed it, in the distance towering Sierra Gador, their faithful barometer.

When the snow begins to fall on its peaks, they know winter has come.

'And look,' Joan said, pointing to where through a gap in the hills to the south-west the sea was shining. 'Sea and mountains, what could be more beautiful.'

'You are right,' said one mother, as wide almost as she was tall. 'You are higher here than we are. We cannot see the sea.'

'And my neighbours?' I asked. 'What do you think of my neighbours?'

Frowning, they followed the direction of my gestures across the *vega*, cultivated land, to the Church of our Virgin of the Sorrows and the cemetery in front of it. '*Vecinos muy tranquilos, muy silenciosos*, very peaceful and silent neighbours,' I added, and they began to laugh.

We turned to the French windows, painted the same blue as the doors and shutters. 'Colour of the heavens,' one woman murmured. 'It pleases me.' We should have realised then that soon there would be a rash of blue doors and window shutters in the village, a colour never used before.

We went through the French windows into the studio. This was an entirely new addition. Below it the donkey shed, on the same level as kitchen and living room, was now a store. The metal roll-up door meant that it could be used as a garage. But only for a very small car, the dirt road outside being too narrow to manoeuvre our autosleeper in.

In the studio, our visitors hardly spared a glance at the tall bookcase crammed with books, the elegant cane easy chairs, well padded for comfort, the two traditional unpainted wooden chairs, the table on which we ate breakfast and lunch in the sunshine, the French windows wide open.

They did, however, like the large settee which could be converted into two separate beds for guests, separate here being an advantage, obviously.

Down over the studio stairs — we should install a handrail, we should need one as we grew older — and through the store to stop at the *cuarto de baño*. Washbasin, mirror, bath and shower, what luxuries . . . And then, look — *un aseo* where you could sit in comfort . . .

This, we knew, was totally unexpected, the first WC to be installed in the village. In answer to an enquiring look, Joan flushed it and they listened entranced to the gushing of the water.

The kitchen, though too small, they decided, was convenient. A good idea, too, that the woman could see the living room and chat to her man if he was home. A rare thing, this, for the men spent all their spare time in the bars, some to drink, some to play cards and dominoes, all to gossip free of the women.

One of the children found the egg cosies. Were they dolls' hats? Our demonstration of how they were used caused a great deal of amusement.

They filed out, still smiling at the ways of *lawingléh* with their eggs. Shook hands with us. Wished us many happy years in our house. Did not formally thank us. Saying thank you was something they rarely if ever did in this village. They gave (very generously) and they received, and that was enough. They did not expect thanks when they gave; that was quite unnecessary. In the same way, they knew they did not need to thank the person who gave them something.

It took a bit of getting used to, but we managed it. It was not long before, in the village, we followed suit.

Soon all our neighbours were having *aseos* installed. Very few indoors; most in outhouses a step or two from the front door. No loo had a seat: more hygienic, they had been assured, to sit on the cold porcelain.

The corrals were now no longer needed. Nor were the stands of prickly pears behind the houses for the minority who had no corral. What a blessing to sit on one's own *aseo* in peace and quiet without risk of being disturbed or overlooked.

One of our visitors had been Carmen, a mason's wife, who lived in the last house in our road, Calle Cruces, The Street of the Crosses. Her husband was deaf, but an excellent lip-reader, so there was never any difficulty in communication.

Her daughter, Carmenita, the diminutive of the name 'Carmen', an attractive redhead with blue eyes and a skin that looked as if it had never been exposed to the sun, arrived at our door.

Her father had finished their new *cuarto de baño*. Her mother would be pleased if we would come and see it.

We said we would be very pleased. Would that afternoon be convenient? Of course: whenever we liked.

Mother Carmen was waiting to greet us at her door. Inside in the small parlour were seated her parents and her three daughters. Her husband, alas, was working away from the village.

On the circular table was a white, elaborately crocheted table-cloth which could only have been part of the mother's bottom drawer. Prospective wives here vied with each other in the size, variety and prettiness of the articles they produced for it.

Two empty chairs were drawn up at the table and we were requested to sit, Carmen using the time-honoured form of words: 'Welcome. My house is your house.'

The home-made doughnuts were hard and heavy. I don't like doughnuts, even good ones, but I had to accept one. I nibbled at it, assuring my anxious hostess it was *muy bueno*.

Baldomero, Carmen's father, rose, went to the big glass-fronted cupboard, the shelves filled with glasses and prettily patterned china, and took out three small cut-glass brandy glasses.

Seated once more, he opened the bottle of brandy with a flourish, filled my glass first and then his own – correct form here, where men take precedence over women in everything – before offering to fill Joan's.

We were flattered. We knew the glass and china were for display to impress relatives and neighbours, and only used on very special occasions.

Joan refused. She said she preferred a cup of coffee.

I saw how pleased Carmen and her daughters were. No village woman drinks. And here was *laingléh* refusing alcohol, behaving as if she were one of them.

Carmenita jumped up to go and make the coffee. Instant it would be, of course, and probably *descafeinado* (the village women were convinced ordinary coffee was bad for the nerves and heart), which Joan doubly disliked.

How glad I was of my brandy. I raised my glass and wished

5

them all health: '*Salud a todo el mundo!*' I drained the glass (it really *was* small); Baldomero promptly following suit. He refilled the glasses. Kept encouraging me to drink up. I needed no encouragement. The frequent brandies were necessary for me to get through the doughnut, which was obligatory. In fact, the more I drank, the better the doughnut tasted.

A good brandy, this Domecq Fundador. The oldest of them all, as well as being one of the driest and least manipulated, no colouring matter being used, so the bodega claims.

Fundador was first marketed in 1874. It owes its existence to a happy accident. In 1850 Domecq shipped a large volume of the raw wine spirit used in making liqueurs, to Amsterdam. The importer refused delivery. The raw spirit was shipped back and remained in the oak casks for several years. When Pedro Domecq Loustea finally tasted it, he was so impressed that he decided to redistil it and sell it. Thus was the first Spanish brandy born.

Carmen waited until we had finished our doughnuts. She stood up decisively, said, 'Now come and see our *cuarto de baño*. All new, the room and all in it.'

She led the way through the front door and around the side of the house to her small patio. There against the wall was a small building constructed of breeze-blocks roughly cemented together.

Carmen opened the door, painted blue we were flattered to see, and gestured: '*Pasen ustedes, por favor.*'

We went in. Stopped. Stared.

The walls from floor to ceiling were covered in pink patterned tiles. They had been put on higgledy-piggledy and there was almost as much plaster to be seen as tile.

The room itself was not quite rectangular, the corners not right angles, the walls drunkenly leaning slightly, the ceiling certainly not horizontal. No matter: the effect was strikingly out of the ordinary, so much so that my feeling was one of dissociation.

In the centre of the room was the pink WC bowl, seatless and, following the example of some of her neighbours, without a cistern. But we had to admit it was pretty. '*Muy bonito,*' we murmured, '*muy bonito.*'

Carmen nodded in agreement. '*Et la ducha,*' she said, pointing.

We looked up. There, carefully positioned directly above the bowl, was the fixed shower head.

We did not dare look at each other; it was important that we kept a straight face.

I turned to Carmen. The family crowded outside the door. I smiled, said enthusiastically, loud enough for them to hear: '*Estupendo, Carmen,*' then addressed myself to the family. 'What a pleasure. Everything well made. Congratulations!'

We stood outside on the patio. Carmen carefully closed the heavenly-blue door. We thanked her most sincerely: we had experienced something we would never forget.

The family chorused the standard reply: '*De nada,* it's nothing.'

Baldomero's eyes were shining with pleasure. '*Otra copita, Alberto, otra copita.*'

It was a statement, almost an order, yet I refused the final glass of brandy, much as I enjoy Fundador.

We left, the ritual good wishes from the entire family following us – 'May you have many years of happiness in your house' – accompanied by much waving and smiles of satisfaction. It was a feather in their caps; the details of our visit would be mulled over again and again with all the neighbours in the *barrio*, not to mention other friends and relatives in the village.

Back in our own *casa*, we luxuriated in our unique experience. Decided there was a promising future in such a time- and-labour-saving idea: surely Carmen and her deaf husband ought to patent it, try to get someone to market it. If not . . .

Some time later, believe it or not, we *did* see in a Spanish paper an article on the same set-up as Carmen's in a minuscule Japanese *cuarto de baño*. Too late again . . .

Later, looking back, we realised that the first significant change in the villagers' way of life was our coming to live among them, with our *aseo, ducha,* and comfortable furniture. Never before had any stranger, let alone an *extranjero*, a foreigner, settled in the village.

What strange customs this *matrimonio*, married couple, had.

Some worth imitating, though, such as the *aseo* and *ducha*, and tap water indoors!

Another example may be mentioned here. Our routine was to walk in the hills for two or three hours each afternoon. We went through the village side by side chatting, often Joan linking her arm in mine and vice-versa.

Some years later, Manolo the Miller, sitting in the sun on the Ramblas wall with some friends, stopped me. 'Alberto,' he said earnestly – we were by now good friends – 'it is not the custom here for a man and wife to walk side by side. The man always goes first, the woman follows. But Juanita and you . . . ?'

I explained as best I could. We were equal partners. We enjoyed each other's company. Spending our time together in our own house, something Manolo and the others found it hard to believe. Yet, as they well knew, I rarely went to the bars, and when I did, it was usually with Joan.

Soon the village knew my reasons. It was not long before man and wife were walking side by side, and later still some *matrimonios*, the young ones especially, were even linking arms or holding hands. Only the gypsies kept to the old way, the woman and her brood following yards behind the man.

And when the telly came, the men had a reason to spend some time at home instead of just using it as a place to sleep and eat.

Joan called me down from the studio. There in the middle of our long, barely-furnished living room was an old crone dressed in the inevitable *luto*, the mourning black. Short of stature, white hair scraped back and tied firmly with a dirty thin white ribbon, sharp features and even sharper eyes, white hairs sprouting from a dark mole on her chin, she held cradled in her arms an enormous fat white rabbit. I saw its pink eyes gaze at me, its pink nose twitch.

Joan said, 'She came in without knocking. Her only words were, "Where is the boss?"'

We smiled at each other. This was the pretence all the villagers shared. In public the husband was always referred to as the boss. His favourite boast was '*Yo mando en mi casa*'. In reality, as

8

everyone knew, it was the woman of the house who gave the orders and was obeyed.

'*Señor*,' said the old woman, unsmiling, utterly ignoring Joan. 'You will buy my rabbit. I reared it myself on the best food.' She dangled it, still as death, by its long pink ears, and I feared for them. 'See how fat it is. Feel.'

I shook my head.

'It is cheap. A good price for you, strangers here, but welcome.'

I shook my head again. 'No, thank you, we do not want the rabbit.'

The old crone's face expressed her incredulity. 'But I have brought it all the way from the Ramblas for you. You *must* want it.'

'No,' I said firmly.

She seemed completely nonplussed. Then her face lit up. '*Aiee*, I know what it is. You cannot kill the rabbit. In your country you go always to the butcher for your meat.' She hardly bothered to hide her contempt. 'That meat. Not fresh like this. I will kill and skin the rabbit for you. The same price.'

'No, *señora*, I do not want the rabbit. We do not like rabbit meat.' (A lie, but justified in the circumstances, I decided.)

'But you have not tried *this*.' By now the poor creature was in the crook of one arm. She prodded it. 'So tender. Much better than chicken. For you I will reduce my price.'

I had deliberately not asked the price. That would have hinted at an interest I did not feel, and would have made my refusal all the more difficult. Besides, I suspected the price for this so-welcome stranger would be at least twice the going rate to her neighbours, and I hated bargaining.

Joan looked at me approvingly for showing such unexpected firmness.

It took me another few firm refusals before the old woman finally gave up. I saw her to the door. '*Adios, señora*, and thank you for the visit.'

Wordless, she stalked away with surprising vigour and did not look back.

'At least' – Joan was smiling somewhat ruefully at me – 'when

9

the word gets about the village, they will know you are not quite the soft touch they probably think you are with your friendly greetings to all and sundry.'

I thought it better not to reply, and she diplomatically changed the subject. 'Do you remember the butcher in the market?'

'I certainly do.'

We had gone to the market to buy some meat. The butcher whose stall Joan stopped at had a good reputation. Joan obviously liked the look of what he had on display. She spent some time deciding what to buy. She finally chose a small lean leg of pork; we thought pork was by far the tastiest meat you could buy here, and the best value; too often the steak and beef was not worth eating.

Joan began to question the butcher, a lean, Moorish-looking man, with a hooked long nose, black hair greased and carefully combed, and an equally carefully cultivated and trimmed moustache.

He ignored her, turned to me. 'What will the *señor* have?' he said, smiling.

The intended compliment was clear: was I not the *jefe*, the boss in my own house?

Joan stepped back as if stung.

I stared the wretched man full in the face and shook my head in plain disgust. '*Vaya, hombre, vaya,*' I said emphatically. I turned away abruptly and hurried to catch Joan up.

'*Vaya*' is such a useful all-purpose word here. Depending on the context and your tone, it can convey anything from admiration through pleasant surprise, approval of someone's wit or action, to utter contempt. I had no doubt at all the butcher got my meaning.

2

The young man we called Gafas because he wore big thick pebbled spectacles came to the door one morning.

Had I any little job I wanted doing?

I had, as a matter of fact. We had not until then spoken except to greet each other in passing. He lived at the other end of the village. All I knew about him was that he already had four children, possessed no land, but never worked as a day labourer in the fields, as did the other landless men.

Tall, thin, unsmiling, tense, I did not take to him. Yet, thinking of his children, I explained what the job was and he agreed to come the next morning.

He came with his wife, as thin as he was and just as tense, to put red polish on the tiles that covered our flat roof, the *terazza*. They worked hard for three hours and we were pleased with the result.

'How much do I owe you?'

'Five thousand *pesetas, señor.*'

'I'm not daft,' I said. 'Nor a visitor. I live here. A peon is paid three hundred and fifty *pesetas* an hour. So I owe you for six hours' work. Two thousand *pesetas.*'

Gafas began to protest vehemently. I cut him short: I hate being done. 'Take it or leave it. You wouldn't want me to tell my neighbours how you tried to cheat me?'

Without another word he snatched the money from my outstretched hand and left. I then noticed that his wife had not waited for him.

Never again, I resolved, would I employ anyone without fixing the price first.

11

Later that week, on a walk up into the hills, we met Gafas on his motorbike. The crate on the carrier was full of grapes. He accelerated when he saw us. Went by so fast on the rutted dirt road that a couple of bunches of grapes spilled out. I called after him, but he did not stop.

It was a very hot afternoon. We had been walking for over an hour and were thirsty. Joan washed the grapes in a nearby stream and we sat down and ate them. Delicious.

The villagers were fond of boasting about it: you could leave your door unlocked all night and all day and nobody would take anything.

Their unfenced land, from which they took three crops a year, was just as safe. Whatever was growing – tomatoes, beans, peas, lettuce, onions, aubergines, artichokes – nobody touched it. The same went for the fig, orange, lemon and banana trees dotted about, even in the remotest places.

Recently, things had suddenly started disappearing. The villagers promptly blamed the gypsies. Nobody from the village would steal. But the *gitanos* . . . There were four gypsy families living in the village now . . . It must be a gypsy.

The *gitanos* were on the surface tolerated, treated like everyone else. They were, though, neither liked nor trusted. They, of course, knew this. Did not mix or attempt to mix with the villagers. Even their children kept themselves to themselves.

The villagers' feelings were quite understandable. Every able-bodied person, male and female, worked in the fields, day in, day out, Gafas being the exception. The *gitanos* never worked. To own land, the ambition of every villager, was to them like being in jail.

'Land!' one *gitano* said to me. 'Land!' He picked up a handful of earth. Tossed it high in the air so that the breeze caught it, blew it away. 'Land! Who would be a slave to land!'

Alfonso, the *gitano* who lived at the top of the village, had 13 children. He did no work other than procreational. I once asked him how he managed to feed and clothe his family. He shrugged, smiled, looked up to the sky, said: 'God clothes and feeds them.' He did, however, sometimes send his wife to work in the fields when, perhaps, God was taking a little time off.

The *gitanos*, then, lived off the land and by their wits. So skilful were they that no one had ever caught them in any wrong doing.

Fodder was very scarce here. Nobody grazed any animal on anyone else's land without permission. When the swarthy, bare-footed *gitano* children led out their goats in the morning, they knew to a metre where they could graze them through the long day; they kept to the edges of the paths. Even when they went up into the hills, they had to be careful. They were not at all popular with the four village goatherds who owned the grazing rights.

The village bee-keeper was called José. He was also the pruner of the vines many villagers grew over their front door, giving them shade in summer, fruit in autumn.

Five kilometres from the village, the hilltops had been planted in pines and eucalyptus. The area was one of José's favoured sites for his 70 or so hives.

It was also one of our favourite walks. One day we saw scrawled in red on the top of each hive: *MUERTE A LOS LADRONES*, Death To The Robbers. This was the first we knew that some hives had been stolen. Then the news reached the village that someone had been robbing the vines farther up the river valley. The village there was famous for its green table grapes, its main crop. Most disturbing of all, the rumour was that it was someone from our village.

There was only one horse in the village. Everyone had a mule or a donkey, but a horse, no. The *gitano* who owned the horse came to live here two years previously. Tall, erect, swarthy, he had a huge handlebar moustache, glossy black curls, perfect white teeth. They dazzled when he smiled, which he did readily.

He was as proud as are all true *gitanos*, and more than proud of his horse; his life seemed to be centred around it. He often grazed it along the edge of the path in front of our house. Sometimes I would pat the shining white animal, nervy, high-spirited, eager, but gentle and utterly obedient, a very Pegasus of an animal. On its back he was as noble as any *hildago* you see in Seville's world-famous fair.

One day I said, 'He's in magnificent condition. What do you feed him on?'

The *gitano* smiled and gestured. 'Grass, as you can see, *señor*. Also hay, oats, milk.'

'Milk? You're joking.'

'No, *señor*, I tell the truth. Milk, yes, milk. He is young, my stallion. He needs milk to grow. He is one of the family. Would you not give your family milk?'

It was on this *gitano* that suspicion fell. Nobody born and bred in the village could be a thief. They had to find a scapegoat. Who better than the *gitano* who owned that horse?

Everyone knew what it cost to keep a horse here. That was why no villager could ever afford to keep one. Where, then, did the *gitano* get the money to keep such an animal, and in such prime condition? Not to mention the five children he had to feed.

Padre Ramón did his best to quell the gossip. 'Whoever the thief is,' he said, 'he will be caught in God's good time. Until then, we must not blame what could be an innocent man.'

This did not go down at all well. Padre Ramón had been the village priest for only three years. What right had he to even suggest the thief was somebody from the village?

Then an old man who lived in an isolated *cortijo* high up in the Sierra came down on his mule on one of his regular trips to get provisions. His bitter complaint in Antonio's bar was that someone had stripped his orange trees, those farthest from the house. He had caught him in the act. Had warned him he would kill him if he caught him again.

Agog, Antonio asked, 'Would you know him again?'

'Of course. Young. Rides a motorbike. Wears glasses. He –'

'Wears glasses?' Antonio interrupted. 'Are you sure?'

The old man pointed a finger at his eyes, a typical gesture here. 'My eyes are still good. I *am* sure. We were face to face. If I catch him again, I will kill him, I swear.'

Neither Antonio nor anyone else in the bar took the old man's threat seriously. They did not tell the old man they knew who

14

the thief was now: what was the point in telling somebody from outside they had a thief in their midst?

The old man finished his wine and left. Manolo the Miller – there was no maize flour like his, so my wife said – smiled and said, 'I know he was a good hunter in his younger days. He is my age now, over eighty. I doubt he still has his shotgun. If he has, it won't fire. Shotguns rust away just as we do.'

It was soon after eight one May morning when the old man came back down from the Sierra. He was leading his mule. Hanging across its back was the body of the young man in glasses.

The mule stopped in front of the mayor's house. By the time the mayor came out, the square was full of silent people, the *gitano* on his white horse towering above them.

The mayor asked for volunteers. Four young men lifted the bloodstained body from the mule's back. Led by the mayor, they carried it into the house. Gafas's wife – or widow as she now was – had already been warned. She stood in the doorway, supported on either side by her father and mother. None of the four children was to be seen.

Bodies cannot be kept in this hot climate. Padre Ramón arrived promptly to arrange the funeral, followed by the Guardia Civil to take the old man away.

The mass was held the next day at eleven in the morning instead of the usual weekday five in the afternoon. Despite this, everyone in the village seemed to be there. The widow, all in black and heavily veiled, was utterly prostrated with grief, crying as noisily as her four children.

The old man was quickly brought to trial, just as quickly released. The judge was quite satisfied his story was true:

'I rose at dawn. I had a premonition. I was certain the thief was coming back. I loaded my shotgun. I hid in the bottom of the orange grove. Soon after first light, he of the glasses appeared. He began to pick my oranges and put them in a sack. I came forward and threatened him. I waved the gun at him. This was to frighten him. I told him it was loaded. He laughed at me. Said I was an old fool. Seized the gun. We struggled. It went off. The shot went into the thief's chest. When I bent to help him up, I found he was dead.'

After the burial, the neighbours called at the widow's house and offered their *pésame*, their condolences. Discreetly they left their gifts of food and money to tide the widow over the next few days, as was the custom.

Imagine, then, the villagers' scandalised feelings when the rumour got about. The widow was going to marry Pepe, he who was not quite right in the head. Who wanted more like him in the village? And the wedding was to be only three months after her husband had been killed. Had the woman no conscience? No feelings? No regard for the customs here? The official mourning time was at least one year, and here was this . . .

Pepe, the widow's new man, was the bee-keeper's son. She and they were next-door neighbours. As Paco the baker, who lived opposite them, pointed out to me: 'What more natural than that they should wish to marry? They have been good friends for some time now. He of the glasses, he who did not like honest work any more than the *gitanos*, went off all day on his motorbike. What more commendable than that José's son, the simple one, should slip over the wall and in through the back door to comfort her. Help her pass the long hours waiting for her husband to come home? You don't have to have much brains for that, do you?'

The rumour died down. The neighbours told themselves that fortunately it was only a rumour.

Suddenly the widow and Pepe disappeared. They had gone to Granada to contract a civil marriage, no marriage at all in the eyes of the villagers. Nor in Padre Ramón's eyes, needless to say.

Five days later, the couple returned and took up residence in the widow's house. That same night, a group of neighbours assembled outside the house. They began what is known here as *la cencerra*. This consists of making as much noise as possible – beating drums, clashing tins and dustbin lids, blowing horns, catcalling. This they kept up for the whole of the next week till after dawn each day.

La cencerra had the desired effect. The couple separated. She went her way, he his.

Two years later, the widow took a lodger – to help keep bread in her four children's mouths, so she averred.

The lodger, a small, swarthy, weasily-looking man, had come to the village to be servant to Roberto and was now without work (see chapter 12).

A lodger only. No question of marriage, a fact for which everyone was thankful.

Nine months later, the widow produced a baby, who grew into a fine fair-haired, blue-eyed boy. *El Comadreja*, The Weasel, as we dubbed him, was swarthy, black-haired, brown-eyed. Consequently, nobody believed he was the father. No one in the village, no male, at any rate, had fair hair and blue eyes. Not even Alberto, *elingléh*. His eyes were stone-colour, and what little hair he now had could never have been fair. Then *who* could be the father?

During the next two years, two more babies arrived, obviously from the same sire, though both were girls. The widow had been watched. She never left the village. Nor, the baker was prepared to swear, did she have any callers while her man was working in the fields. Her man *must*, then, be the father!

The baker shook his head in disbelief at his own assertion. But were he not the father, why else would he have changed character. Now be working all day and every day? With a good reputation as a peon, willingly hired by the landowners?

Certainly he *was* a changed character. A listener now, not a loud-mouthed talker in Antonio's bar. No longer a drunkard. Content with his *café solo*. Both the widow and he had put on weight. They looked and acted as a happily married couple. And Gafas's eldest girl mothered the new family devotedly.

The youngest five of Alfonso the *gitano*'s 13 children play quietly in the dust in front of their white one-storey house. As we approach, they stop. We stop also. We stare at each other; no words are exchanged; here in our village such open curiosity is natural. We smile, our satisfaction mutual.

On this February evening, the sun and slanted shadows still lie warm on the rags that only partly conceal their lean brown bodies. The youngest, a tiny boy (he can't be more than two), leaves the others, comes gravely forward, naked except for one very large shoe, halts face to face with me, gravely offers the well-chewed end of his sugar cane. I accept, take a token chew, hand it back.

He nods, studies the end of the sugar cane for a moment, lifts his head, shows his white teeth in a wide smile, turns, drags his shoe back to where the other *gitanillos* are standing, watchful, motionless and silent.

I lift my hand and we resume our walk up the steep path into the hills.

A cloud of tawny dust rises, shrouds the scene momentarily and hides from our view river bed, surrounding hills, the white humble faces of the little houses.

The dust is so dry the lightest breeze will lift it, send it searching into your mouth, your eyes, your hair. '*Una pena*, this dust, it dries out the lungs, especially we old men. Worse than the summer flies,' Nicolas says, and coughs, the sound dry as the dust itself.

This breeze as suddenly dies away as it sprang up, drops the dust from its hands, reveals gathered on the bare baked earth the huge circus tent, the wagons, the canvas-roofed carts, all drawn up in a bright circle around it.

A black-moustached man, bandana poppy-bright, smiling bends to put down a bowl of food for the puppy tied to the wheel of his cart: the puppy's joyous tail wags its whole body.

The *gitano* children roam about, their dogs and goats as glad to move as they. Women in yellow and green and blue and scarlet prepare the meal, their hair, black as almond trunks, but shining in the midday sun, falls freely to their waist, or is plaited, the entwined ribbons echoing the colours of their dresses.

Horses, mules, donkeys wander, trying to find something to graze upon.

Near one painted wagon, village boys and girls stand silent. The cage has black bars, thick and strong. It is so small the bear, grey as age, has hardly room to turn; the fur is gone from his flanks and back.

Like some mute automaton, he shifts his sad weight from paw

to paw, his head ticking in time from side to side. Nearby, the indifferent gypsies are now feeding, content and at ease in the soothing shade.

3

We did not realise when, on a sudden impulse, we bought the house, how many advantages there were living in the village: pure serendipity, in which (the perpetual triumph of hope over experience?) I have always believed.

The major advantage is the climate. The village, five kilometres from the sea, is set above a flat-bottomed valley, the cultivated *vega*, surrounded by hills. This gives us a delightful micro-climate. No measurable rainfall, for a start. The huge dark clouds that in winter we often see advancing from the north-east pass on the other side of Sierra Gador and drop their rain on the fortunate fields there.

In winter, also, we have some cool cloudy days. In the evening we light the *estufa*, the gas fire, after we have closed the shutters over the glassless windows. The normal winter weather, however, is blue skies and sun, the temperature during the day being that of an agreeably hot summer's day in England.

In summer, the heat can be intense but bearable, provided you more or less follow the pattern the villagers follow.

The men go to work in the fields at 6 a.m. or earlier, come home at midday, eat their *almuerzo*, their main meal, then take their siesta from, say, 2 to 5.30 p.m. It is during the siesta, the men assure you, that many children are conceived.

The men do another three hours' work. From the fields they go straight to the bar. Home again at midnight or later, they eat a light supper, then relax out of doors for a while before turning in.

The cool sea breeze in the summer evenings brings welcome relief; it is then we dine, having eaten little in the middle of the day. Women with their young children go to and fro to the shops. There they congregate, purchases forgotten for the time being.

All their neighbours are out of doors. Old men sit outside; women brush the dust from their doors, a perpetual losing battle; children play noisily.

Going to the shops (their larders) is an important ritual. A couple of hundred yards often takes an hour or more; no neighbour must be passed without a chat. As the evening wears on, the women sit on their *terrazas* or in front of their doors. They talk incessantly: there is always so much to talk about.

On some summer days, go out of doors and the heat strikes you as if it were something palpable. Unless you really have to be elsewhere, the only place to be is indoors.

On such days, we more than ever bless the fact that we did not heed the advice of those, Juan White Mule being the most insistent, who said it would be cheaper and better to tear the old house down and put in its place a modern chalet like those the foreigners over the hill live in.

Our metre-plus thick cob-and-stone walls were built to keep out the heat. Close the door and shutters and the living room remains cool and shady, whereas, as we know, in those chalets over the hill there is no place to hide from the heat.

All the village houses are built like ours. The villagers do not want the sun in their rooms, even in winter, or bright light, either; winter as well as summer, they prefer to live in the shade. At night, too, their naked light bulbs are of so low a wattage they give no more light than a candle or two. No one reads, so who wants a bright (and expensive) light?

Doors and shutters closed, you are protected from the hottest day. Make sure also that before summer comes, your bright beaded curtains are in position in front of your door, and that behind your window bars there are no holes in your fine-mesh flyscreens, and you will be protected from the summer flies as well.

(Better, needless to say, not to be here during July and August. A little place in the sierras, perhaps? Or, if nothing else presents itself, enjoying the English so-called summer.)

Living as we do some distance from the sea and encircled by

21

hills has another climatic advantage: we are mostly spared the winter winds, often gale force, which so frequently ravage the coast. They rise suddenly, and as suddenly fall, a welcome feature. But when they are blowing, they are most unpleasant because, though rarely what we would call cold, they whip up the blinding dust that lies everywhere, and no one would choose to be out in them.

We bought our house on a sudden impulse, as I've said; a stupid thing to do. In the event, however, serendipity being with us, it turned out to be one of the best things we ever did.

We had planned to spend the winter in our caravan wandering along Spain's south coast. We had a puncture one Sunday afternoon just west of Almería. Four hours later, I returned with the caravan wheel. Puncture mended, no; new tyre, provided as a great favour, yes.

Tired out, as darkness fell, we decided to pull into a camp for the night. There we stayed for our allotted four months, we so liked it and the neighbouring town, its life centred on its busy fishing fleet.

On the camp I swopped English lessons for Spanish with Alfredo from the town two kilometres down the road. He taught English there; his accent and lack of grasp of English idiom had to be heard to be believed.

This is par for the course. When Spain finally decided to put its money on English rather than French as the second language, it simply instructed its language teachers to teach English as well as, or as an alternative to, French.

What could the majority of teachers do except attempt to mug up enough English from grammar and course books? Result: whatever else they achieved, they had little ability to speak it.

Alfredo at least wanted to improve. I have often tried to engage his English-teaching colleagues in conversation. Always they smile, carefully explain to me they have had no practice in speaking English and are too shy to try with what they call in their good Andalusian dialect *uningléh*.

One day we accepted Alfredo's oft-repeated invitation to go

with him to the village (now *our* village) where he was born and brought up: we simply had to meet his relatives.

It was our first experience of village houses and village hospitality – doughnuts, brandy and fruit in each house we visited.

Alfredo's uncle, Miguel, a little, spry 82-year-old, took us into his garden. Showed us his fruit trees, his potato patch, his beans, his lettuce, his onions.

Agile as a monkey, he shinned up a banana tree and picked us a hand of bananas. Down again, he repeated the performance on a lemon and orange tree.

Isabel, his wife, watched from her sharp slanted eyes as I began to peel one of the oranges. Rose impatiently. Seized the orange. Fetched a long sharp knife. Made a perfect monkey tail of the skin. Handed the orange back to me, her contempt for this foreigner who did not even know how to peel an orange plain in her face and movements.

We made the slow rounds of the other relatives. In one of the dusty village bars we met Antonio, Alfredo's first cousin. While we drank beer, I from the bottle as did the other men, Joan from a glass produced with a flourish and dusted again by her before she drank, we saw the cousins in deep conversation.

Suddenly Alfredo turned, said in his charmingly risible English, 'I've just bought my cousin's house. In the best part of the village, with the best view. Do you want to buy it?'

'Ah, at how many hundred per cent profit?' I said.

'No, for what I have just given for it. Truly.'

'How much, then?'

The price in *pesetas* he gave us was at that time the equivalent of £350.

I saw the look on Joan's face. Hurriedly I demanded what on earth did we want a house in this village for? As well as our own house, we had a house which had belonged to my mother in St Ives. Enough, wasn't it? St Ives. An ideal place to go on spending time whenever we felt like it.

'Yes, if the town was thatched,' said Joan tartly, turning one of my favourite jokes against me. To Alfredo she said: 'Yes, I'd like to see the house.'

My heart sank.

23

The property, with its donkey shed next door, its big corral for the pigs, goats, rabbits and hens, big enough to make into a self-contained flat if ever we got around to it, on the hillside behind the *terraza*, was much larger than we had expected.

'It was once three houses. Three families were brought up here,' Alfredo said.

Up to then we had no intention whatsoever of buying any property, but Joan at once decided this was an offer we could not refuse. Considering the price, what was a few thousand spent on it to make it as we wanted it? If we didn't like it, we could always sell it, couldn't we?

'Can I walk on the *terraza*, Alfredo?'

'Of course.'

I put a cautious foot on it. Felt it begin to give way. Stepped back just in time to prevent myself falling through. Looked at Joan appealing. Was this ruin what she really wanted to own?

Unimpressed, she turned to Alfredo. 'I'll buy it.'

'I'm glad,' he said, and they shook hands.

Motion carried by the usual majority of one.

That, as far as we were concerned, was that, such was our naïvité.

It was only after we had spent the money putting the house right and adding the studio that we met a bank manager holidaying in the area and exploring the village. We told him our story. Too good to keep to ourselves, wasn't it?

He and his new wife agreed. 'And the deeds?' he asked. 'You have the deeds, of course? This house is worth quite a sum now. It will be worth much more when you come to sell it. But you must have the deeds.'

He could not hide his incredulity when we told him we had no deeds. He earnestly advised us to get them as soon as possible. Without the deeds we had no right to the property. Suppose the owner reclaimed it? He certainly could in law – we did not even have a receipt for what we had paid him.

After a prolonged search, Antonio, Alfredo's cousin, found the *escritura* and willingly handed it over. But whose name was this on it? Not his, certainly.

The name, Fernandez, was that of the previous owner, or the

owner before that, I never found out. Fernandez was first cousin to Antonio's father. No need, therefore, to have paid good money to those lawyer robbers to have had a new *escritura* drawn up. And surely now, Alfredo's friends being *his* friends, we could rest content with the old *escritura*?

We said we preferred to have the matter settled legally.

Antonio shrugged. Said he would get Alfredo – was he not a schoolmaster? – to write a *papel*, a paper, signed by Fernandez, who fortunately was still alive, to say we had bought the property. Then he, Antonio, would sign it, and that would be that.

It took us another year to get a new *escritura* drawn up in Berja, 11 kilometres away. It was the official's job also to fix the rent.

The official studied the Fernandez *escritura* through his large black horn-rimmed glasses, thoughtfully fingering his splendid black beard. He eventually looked at us, a trifle pityingly, I thought. Was it because we certainly did not have the affluent appearance of most foreigners who came to his office? Or was it because of the *escritura*? Or that it was only a village house?

He blinked at us, said quietly, 'It is a very small village *casa*.'

I instantly fervently agreed. Realised this assessment of his would work to our benefit. Wondered how precisely he had come to this conclusion. Could it be that Fernandez's *escritura* was for only one of the three original houses?

Whatever the reason, who was I to attempt to enlighten a functionary of the state, to whom still clung vestiges of the absolute power such people had vested in them in Franco's time?

He sighed. 'A very small *casa*.'

'But a bit better than a caravan.'

'True.' He smiled, his glasses catching the light from the dusty, closed window to his left. 'A *small* caravan. The *casa* is small. It is only fitting that your rent be also. I will prepare the new *escritura*. You can collect it in a fortnight.'

We shook hands cordially and left, I congratulating myself on my still tongue. And when the rent assessment arrived, so small we could not believe our luck, I felt inordinately proud of my business prowess, up to then conspicuously lacking, as well as

25

– I must confess – a bit of a trickster. Something, I hasten to add, I managed to live with.

Two other strokes of good fortune merit mention, but a digression first.

We had boycotted Spain during Franco's dictatorship. After his death, our first visit to spend Joan's winnings on Ernie was to Madrid, principally to go to the Prado to view the works of El Greco, Velásquez (his *Las Meninas* in particular) and Goya, though drinking wine in the sunshine at a café table from time to time in the monumental Plaza Mayor put the seal on an unforgettable experience.

The next visit, also provided by a benevolent Ernie, was to a beachside hotel a few kilometres from Marbella. There in February, we swam and lazed in the open air to our heart's content.

The result of these two visits was quite unexpected. One day Joan came home, told me she had sold her car and bought a caravan: a continental model, fortunately, the door opening on the safe side of the road, i.e. the right.

Two days to pack and we hitched up and set off for Spain, never having towed a caravan before.

The messes we got ourselves in! One will forever remain with us. An October sandstorm near Benidorm; visibility only a few yards as night fell. I gratefully found a space to pull off the road. Tired out, we began to settle down for the night. Thunderous knocking. We opened the door. A wizened Spaniard ordered us off his land, weight being added to his ravings by the shotgun he was waving at me.

A little farther on, I turned off the road down a narrow track which passed under a bridge. Stopped. Praying there would be no traffic. Was there room to pass? Didn't know for sure, the blinding stinging sand made it impossible to see.

We slept well enough. Woke to a windless blue sky. We went out to breathe the fresh air. And there, literally only five yards in front of us, was the cliff edge with a 50-foot drop to the rocks below . . .

But back to our house and the further two strokes of luck.

We found when we enquired about putting the house to rights that the housing regulations from Franco's time were still in force: only slight alterations were permitted. Through Alfredo's good offices, we employed a small builder. He would do what we wanted, including what was essential – putting a new room (the studio) on top of what was formerly the donkey shed. As far as he was concerned, all the work consisted of permitted alterations. But – and it was a big but – no contract, no bills, no receipts; only *dinero*, cash, was to change hands regularly as the work progressed.

It was slow work, his men only appearing when other jobs permitted, but it went well enough. We lived in the caravan on the camp and visited the site on and off to see how things were going. This rogue of a builder, whose name meant 'Sunday', believe it or believe it not, was undoubtedly diddling us, but we accepted this was fair enough in view of the circumstances.

To do the wiring, Alfredo found us a young man employed by the local private telephone company, who supplemented his wage by a bit of moonlighting. He did an expert job at a price much less than we had expected.

'Why so cheap?' I anxiously asked Alfredo.

'Do not worry. The work is first class. It is just that he gets his materials very cheaply.'

I thought it wiser not to enquire further.

It was a great moment when the young man, as if to prove what Alfredo said, proudly switched all the lights on and off, including the two-way switches to bedroom and studio.

He also insisted on testing the power points, positioned where Joan had instructed him.

Perhaps he told me where the electricity supply was coming from. I couldn't swear to it: I never pay attention to such mundane matters.

The result was (and here at last we come to the first stroke of luck, not before time, you may think) that we had free electricity for five years.

It was only then that an old man and his young assistant came to read the meter.

I said we had no meter.

The old boy was so startled that his specs jerked off and hung from one ear.

'*Hombre!*' he exploded. '*Imposible.* You must have a *contador.*'

Despite my repeated denials, he insisted on searching for it.

Completely foxed, he asked where did I get my supply from? On the *terraza* his incredulity knew no bounds as he spied the wire linking us to his firm's wires passing overhead.

'*Hombre!* What danger. Who did this? It is our electricity you are using.' Furiously he brandished his pliers. 'I must cut you off.'

This was an emergency. A glance at Joan and she dashed down and brought up the bottle of Fundador and three brandy glasses. By then I had put the chairs on the *terraza*, but in the shade, of course, close to the bedroom wall.

I asked them to sit. Poured generously from the bottle. Carefully explained how ignorant I was about such esoteric matters.

'You see, *señor*,' I said deprecatingly, 'I am only a writer. I know about pen and paper, and that is all. Yet, as I tell my neighbours, I prefer the pen to the spade.'

My explanation seemed completely to satisfy my interrogator. Had what I said neatly fitted in with his stereotype of a writer and how he behaves? Whatever the reason, the brandy did its work; the oftener he drained his glass, the more benevolently disposed towards us he became.

Did we promise to come to the office tomorrow and sign the contract? I solemnly promised. Good. Then in that case he would not cut us off. In a day or two his colleague would come and install the *contador*, then all would be as it should be.

He refused another brandy. Rose slightly unsteadily; his young assistant, who had drunk only the one glass, kept a watchful eye.

His boss breathed in deeply, then out came the formula: 'May you have many happy years in your house.'

Our second stroke of luck followed exactly the same pattern.

By what we supposed was only a coincidence, a man came

soon after the electricity man to read the water meter. There *was* no water meter. The same incredulous bewilderment. Why had no one come to read the meter before? How was I, a foreigner and only a simple writer trying to earn my bread, to know?

The phrase I used, *tratando de ganar mi pan y cebolla*, trying to earn my bread and onion, tickled his fancy, referring as it did to the time when, during and after the Civil War, bread and onions were, according to the villagers, about all they had to eat, Franco having cut off their supply of water from the Sierra Nevada as a punishment for their being Republicans and fighting against him.

We parted cordially. He assured me that soon someone would come to install the *contador* and all would be well.

The water meter was duly installed. This measured the water used *inside* the house. Not, however, the separate supply up above at the back of the studio where our thoughtful rogue of a builder had put the *pila*, the big stone sink and draining board, so that my woman could follow the custom of the village women and wash her clothes in water which, even in winter, is never cold, and in summer tepid or warm.

The man who installed the meter indoors was well content – had he not carried out his orders to the letter?

My attitude was the same as before. Who was I to interfere and suggest that he should, perhaps, also be metering the water used at the *pila*, far more, need it be said, than Joan used in the house? Best let sleeping dogs lie.

Three or four years later, the pipe supplying the sink sprang a leak. The water bubbled up on the path between Patricio Pastor's house and ours.

How to get a plumber to come from the nearby town? Any you asked would immediately solemnly promise to come *mañana*, tomorrow. You would be lucky if they turned up a week, a fortnight, a month, later; but probably they would *never* show up.

Patricio's advice was to go and see *el del agua*, he of the water, in the town hall.

Hardly was I back home than two workmen arrived in their ramshackle van. They gazed thoughtfully at the leak. Said it was serious. Requested politely that I turned off the water.

I said I could not. But I must have a stopcock in the house? I had, but unfortunately it did not control this water.

They looked at me wonderingly. Here was another mad foreigner. Would I nevertheless try? Of course. One watched me; the other contemplated the water. It still bubbled up as strongly as before.

Now they eyed me suspiciously before setting to work to dig up the path to find both the ancient stopcock and the leak. I congratulated them and hastily retired indoors.

Job finished, they told me they had connected the outside supply to the inside so that now *all* the water we used would be metered.

I agreed. Said that was what should have been done in the first place. Offered them a brandy.

They refused. They did not drink alcohol while they were working. I saw from their eyes and unsmiling faces what they thought of me. I was glad to get shot of them.

From now on we would be paying for every drop of water we used. As the older of the two said before they left, looking me in the eye: '*Hay que pagar el agua que se gasta, verdad,*' We must pay for the water we use, isn't that so?

The electricity story did not have a happy ending.

We decided to change the standard village wattage from 110 to 220 so that we could use an electric fire and kettle.

The firm's office in the nearby town was dingy and depressing, lit by a single naked low-wattage bulb, a perfect example of the cobbler's children being the worst shod.

I took an instant dislike to the man behind the counter. As I listened to the curt, unsmiling way he dealt with the three people in front of me in the queue, my dislike grew. Here was one of the old school: an unrepentant Falangist who was acting, new democracy or no new democracy, as he had always acted – as if his position and power were still unchallengeable. One of the many who lamented the passing of Franco's Fascist government.

He reminded me of another such, a grizzled weasel of a man,

a counter clerk in the post office, so ignorant he used a calculator to find out how much ten stamps at, say, 45 pesetas, came to. A good party member – he was always eager to tell you so – his job a permanent reward for services rendered.

I kept my feelings to myself as I asked the man in the electricity office how much it would cost to change the wattage. He gave me a figure, a not inconsiderable sum. Told me to come back in three days; the documents would be ready for me to sign, then the change could be effected.

When I went back, I found the price he now asked was exactly twice what he had given me previously.

Why? Because the company had put it up the day after he had given me the old price, that was why. He smirked at the people queuing behind me: these foreigners were always kicking up a fuss, weren't they?

I seized the chance to have a good row; by now my old rugby blood was up. I had worked hard to acquire a more than adequate armoury of abusive, not to say coarse, words and expressions, as I had done years ago in French. (How otherwise can you give vent to your feelings in such situations?)

I let loose. He blenched, rendered speechless, perhaps, by surprise at my vocabulary. His eyes flickered at the people behind me, now hugely enjoying the fracas. He had lost face, that was obvious; none of his clients, at least not the sort of clients assembled here, would have dared speak to him as this foreigner – English, of course, *uningléh!* – had done.

Yet he knew he held the trump card. Told me with what dignity he could muster that if I wanted the change, that was the price the company was asking, take it or leave it.

I took it. Signed up. Paid up with all the ill grace I could summon, muttering a few more insults, among which the words 'scandal' and 'robbers' figured prominently.

The functionary ignored this. Stiffly he informed me that one of his men would be around *mañana* (fatal word) to do what was necessary.

I surprised him again by offering my hand which, after a second's hesitation, he took.

I left, the approving glances of the people in the queue behind me following me out. Joan, as was her custom in such familiar situations, had slipped out quietly when I began my tirade. She did not wish to hear my story; was she going to get the new wattage or not?

I said she was. But when? That was a question I could not answer. I felt sure the man would wreak his revenge by keeping us waiting and waiting. She said she didn't wonder, after the exhibition I'd indulged in.

To my utter and gratified surprise, a man came the next day, as had been promised: my 'exhibition' must have had some effect, after all. The man's unexpected arrival almost made me revise my opinion of the Fascist in the office.

The house that Miguel, Alfredo's 82-year-old uncle, and Isabel, his wife live in, the house we visited the day Joan bought our *casa*, is the grandest in the village. The front looks out on Calle Principal, the main street; the huge high-ceilinged living room with its great window at the back onto Miguel's vegetable plot, and the *vega* with the almost perpetually dry river bed stretching through it to the distant sea, a splendid peaceful view.

In the plot and directly beneath the house wall, Miguel grows his row of banana trees; the bananas always ripen well, because they are in full sun and sheltered from the wind.

His orange and lemon trees are planted here and there haphazardly among the vegetables he grows for the house, and for his less-fortunate relatives and friends – potatoes, onions, lettuce, cauliflower, cabbage, tomatoes, runner beans, French beans, aubergines. No sweetcorn, broad beans, fond though he is of them, or peas; he knows they are a waste of time; they do not do well here. Recently, however, he's taken his friend Paco's advice and successfully grown mangetout; both wives (both are Isabel) love to see the purple-red flowers more than eating the pods, reason enough to grow the plants.

When Isabel married Miguel, her dowry was a tiny house in Calle Real that they were to live in, with enough money as well to buy new furniture, fittings, linen, china, cutlery.

Beginning, of course, with the *cama matrimonio*, the matrimonial bed. This would be proudly displayed to relatives and neighbours when they came to baptise the house. How Isabel longed to hear the words addressed to her that she herself had addressed so often to other brides: 'May you have many years of enjoyment of it.'

Early one morning Miguel prepared to set off with the dowry money to Berja.

'Miguel,' Isabel said, looking him earnestly full in the face, 'you will remember the thing you have promised?'

Miguel gestured his astonishment at the question. 'Of course, Isabel, why should I not?'

Isabel watched him kick the reluctant mule into a shambling trot. Did she have misgivings even then of entrusting the thick wad of 5,000-*peseta* notes to him, knowing full well his fatal weakness? Or did she believe their marriage would be proof against it?

Evening came, and it grew later and later. Isabel stood motionless in her doorway. It was a beautiful sunset; she did not notice it; she was too busy scanning the winding Berja road.

At last the mule came over the brow of the hill. Miguel was riding like an old man, back bent, head lowered. One look was enough for Isabel. She turned, went indoors, shutting the door quietly behind her.

She sat stiffly at the kitchen table and folded her arms across her bosom. At last, Miguel entered and crept to the only other chair. Isabel waited in silence, staring at him, her eyes never leaving his face.

She could hardly hear him when he began to speak.

'I met Uncle Paco in Berja, and—'

'That nobody, that drunkard!'

'Yes ... well, I ... we—'

'You told him you had the money?'

Miguel nodded.

'And your purpose?'

'Yes, well ... Uncle Paco said I could make it into a much greater sum. With my winnings I could buy you jewels – real pearls and diamonds.' Miguel looked at his wife for the first time, said pleadingly: 'I thought, *querida*, how beautiful you

33

would look in . . .' He did not finish the sentence: the stony look on his wife's face was enough to silence him.

'And you come back with nothing?'

'Nothing.'

'Then how can I bear to look my neighbours in the eye? And you –'

'I know, I know. I have lost face. They will mock me,' Miguel cried. 'That I cannot bear . . . But I already know what I must do. I have made up my mind.'

Isabel listened in silence to his plan. She raised no objection, indeed seemed glad he was going.

Who could blame her? Miguel certainly did not. He would make it up to her, that he swore on his mother's grave. More than make it up to her, no matter how long it took.

Miguel was more than glad when he arrived in Cuba. The crossing had been rough, the boat small and cramped; and he was a very poor sailor.

He had relatives in Havana, the capital. The language was no problem; and living under one dictator was much the same as living under another: keep a still tongue, be blind to all that did not directly concern you, and work, work, work. What's more, all his relatives were making money, all living on very little, all saving hard, all longing for the day they had saved enough to come home and retire, basking in their neighbours' admiration, even though tinged with envy, the stronger, the better.

Miguel was in luck. He found a job at once in a big store. The boss was a bachelor in his fifties, of pure Andalusian descent. He and Miguel took to each other at once. Miguel put in the long hours demanded, willingly and without complaint. Within five years he was chief assistant. He had a peasant shrewdness, though he could not write with ease, and an excellent head for figures. In another two years he was cashier.

One day his boss took him to one side and confided in him. 'The business is thriving, Miguelito, as you know. Yet I am not a rich man. In fact, I am in grave financial difficulties.'

Miguel's face betrayed his complete astonishment. 'Surely not, *don* Fernando. I cannot believe it.'

'I am, Miguel, I am. And all because of the fatal weakness.'

34

Women, thought Miguel at once, but he prudently kept silent.

His boss seemed to read his thoughts. 'No, Miguel, it's not that. It's that I'm a compulsive gambler. I *must* gamble. I've tried to stop. I cannot. I've lost a great deal of money over the years. So far, though, I've always been able to keep out of debt.'

He was silent for such a long time, Miguel thought the conversation was over.

'Now, Miguelito, things are getting worse. I've got in with a rich crowd. We're playing for higher and higher stakes.'

'Why not back out, *don* Fernando?' Miguel said; but even as he asked the question, he knew the answer.

'I can't, Miguel, I can't. If I do, I shall lose face, that I cannot bear.' He grimaced, as if at his own stupidity, and sighed deeply. 'Now my fear is . . . can you guess what my fear is, Miguel?'

Miguel knew only too well what his boss's fear was, yet he did not venture to say.

'I can see from your face you know. Yes, my fear is, I shall gamble away my business . . . So, after many sleepless nights, I have found a way of avoiding the risk.'

'Well done, *don* Fernando. But if you cannot withdraw from this rich group you speak of, then how are you going to do it?'

'You know I trust you completely. We are like brothers.'

'I know, and I am honoured.'

'Then I shall avoid the risk by putting the business in your name.'

'In my name, *don* Fernando?' Miguel was not sure he had heard correctly, and could only stare in utter amazement at his boss.

'Yes, Miguel. Then, whatever my losses, they cannot take my business to pay my debts.'

It was with the greatest reluctance that Miguel agreed; but if this was what *don* Fernando really wanted . . .

The legal formalities were soon completed, and the business was Miguel's.

Ten years to the day that Miguel landed in Cuba, his boss died suddenly of a heart attack. After the funeral, Miguel sold the business and headed for home.

What prestige he would have in the village; a penniless man

back now with a fortune, still in his mid-thirties and never needing to do another day's work.

Isabel. He would buy the big house in Calle Principal she had always wanted. He would make Juan, the owner, his first cousin, an offer he could not refuse. Juan and his wife were getting old. Their house was now too big for them. They could have his house in Calle Real; it would be just right. And he would put a substantial sum of money in their pocket, enough for them to live out their days without worries. What a joy it would be to Isabel to be installed as mistress of the finest house in the village. And what a triumph for him.

Shortly after Miguel arrived back, he and Isabel moved into the new house. Isabel had been genuinely pleased with the jewels he had brought her – pearls and diamonds – and immediately asked him what he thought the neighbours would say.

She was even more pleased when he said she could have whatever she wished to furnish the new house. Everything new, if that was what she wished; money was no problem. And – this he would insist on – the grandest matrimonial bed anyone in the village had ever seen.

'Alberto,' Nicholas said when he had finished telling me the quite incredible story, 'the neighbours watched as all the new things were delivered to the house. Never had they seen such costly things.'

Here Nicholas made a dramatic pause (all these old men are great storytellers).

'When Miguel went to Cuba, his woman gave the matrimonial bed to her younger sister, who was soon to get married. So the one thing they noticed while the new things were being delivered was that there was no *cama matrimonio*. Two single beds only, put on Isabel's orders into two separate bedrooms.'

Nicholas sighed and shook his head, but the look on his face conveyed quite a different message.

'Poor Miguel. Just imagine, Alberto, all these years, Isabel still a beautiful woman, very beautiful . . . Poor Miguel, there he was dying of thirst sitting by a sparkling stream and forbidden for ever to drink!'

4

Every Spaniard, male and female, has two surnames. In the family Díaz, for instance, the husband's name is Ricardo Díaz Rodríguez. Díaz is his father's surname, Rodríguez, his mother's.

The wife's name is Eloise Jiménez Rosada, Jiménez being her father's surname, Rosada, her mother's.

You refer to them formally as *los señores* Díaz, or more familiarly, *la familia* Díaz. When using their Christian names, *don* or *doña* put in front of them is a mark of respect.

The villagers began by addressing us as *señor* and *señora*, then as *don* Alberto and *doña* Juanita, but they soon dropped this as we became friends. The only ones who persisted in using *don* and *doña* were Paco the baker and his family, even after we became good friends. But they were *foresteros*, strangers, who came from a town 12 kilometres away. They had lived in the village for 20 years, but *foresteros* they would forever remain.

We had resolved not to burden our memory with all these names; we would use only their Christian names. The trouble was that here by far the most popular names were Paco (short for Francisco) and Maria, sometimes shortened to Mari: how would we tell them apart?

At baptism, the Marias were usually given another name: Mari Sol, Mari Isabel, Mari Carmen, Mari Conchita – but these were dropped when they reached marriageable age, thus joining all the other Marias or Maris.

We decided nicknames were the answer. Mrs Thatcher we so named because she bore a striking resemblance, though of course not nearly so superbly groomed, to *La Dama de Hierro*, The

Iron Lady, as the villagers delightedly and admiringly called the original.

Our Mrs Thatcher was in charge of the village market. The great barn-like building, empty save for a few trestle-tables, was where Mrs Thatcher sold her *carne* – chicken and rabbits.

The morning we went to buy a chicken, she had only a few pieces of meat left. Would they do? No? Then '*Vamos,*' let's go.

Her house was nearby. She opened the corral door and took out four hens. She placed them in a line in front of us. To our surprise, they crouched there, looking as pathetic as if they knew what was going to happen.

'You choose. I will kill, pluck and clean it now, and my daughter will bring it to your house.'

I told her I would rather she chose. Added weakly that they all looked alike to me.

She glanced at me, puzzled. '*Seguro?*' she said.

I told her I *was* sure. She replied she would choose the best for me, her *amigo*.

We were glad to hurry away.

Soon Mrs Thatcher retired and her buxom daughter-in-law, Clotilde, took over; no need to give her a nickname – she was the only Clotilde in the village.

She had pork as well as chicken and rabbit on offer. 'Killed yesterday. One of our own pigs,' she said proudly.

The village woman she was serving left. Clotilde appeared uneasy. I asked her what was the matter.

'We are here alone. *Muy comprometido*, very compromising.'

Unbelievable. I could not help laughing. Very compromising with the big double doors and the shutters wide open!

'Wait,' I cried, 'wait until I have closed the doors and shutters.'

She blushed, and this made her appear all the more attractive.

Three women came in. Clotilde, spared further embarrassment, became her normal outgoing self, lively and assured.

She weighed my pork.

'What are those?' I said incredulously, pointing.

'My inheritance from my mother-in-law,' she said, playing her willing part. This *ingléh*, she knew, had a sense of humour similar to the villagers'; ever ready for a laugh, he was. Already, he had adopted one of their favourite sayings: *La vida pasa mejor con un chiste*, Life goes better with a joke.

'*Mi herencia*, these stones, they are accurate. My mother-in-law has used them for years.'

The stones were of different shapes and sizes, but all were as smooth with much handling as if water-worn.

'But –'

'The iron weights were lost long ago. These stones serve in their place. The man from the town council –'

The rest of her remark was drowned by my bellow of laughter. A moment more and Clotilde and the three women joined in.

Our neighbour two doors up is called Juan. This is a name almost as common as Paco. Juan has a white mule, of which he is inordinately proud. It is the only one in the village, so (of course) we named him Juan White Mule.

'*Un animal noble*,' he used to say. 'I mount him and he knows where to go – he reads my thoughts. Gentle, also. My little granddaughter rides him. He waits for her to tell him where to go . . . *Un animal noble*.'

I patted the mule's sturdy neck; the dust rose in a cloud. Obviously unused to such treatment, he tossed his head and curled back his lips, revealing yellow teeth.

It was, therefore, a complete surprise when I saw Juan White Mule approaching on a brown mule. I lifted my hands, fingers spread, the typical questioning gesture; no need for words.

Juan pulled at the single rein, made of woven esparto grass. He nodded. 'Yes, Alberto, I had to sell my white mule. He was getting too old for work.'

'But –?'

He nodded again. Smiled conspiratorially. 'Yes, I know. The mule did not look his age. His teeth, too, did not betray him.' He chuckled with satisfaction. 'I sold him to a man in a *cortijo*, farm, in the Sierra. A good bargain. We were both satisfied.'

'And did you tell him how old the mule was?'

'He did not ask. He preferred to judge for himself.' Juan's look told me clearly he thought I was mad to ask such a question.

He waited for me to say something; I felt it wiser to keep silent. I knew Juan's reputation as a shrewd businessman. Had he not once been foreman of the nearby sugar factory, now only a ruin, when all that was grown in the *vega* was sugarcane?

'A young mule, this one,' said Juan. 'It was the mule of Louis, he of the *plazeta*, little square – *qué descanse en paz*, may he rest in peace. And what would his widow want with a mule now that she has no man? She is my first cousin. To help her, I offered to buy the mule. She was pleased to sell it to me at my price.'

He sighed deeply. 'Poor Louis. Not old. Not nearly as old as I . . . But who can tell when we are called? Life, Alberto, is a short dream.'

He kicked the mule into a trot. Called cheerily: 'He moves well, this young mule. I shall get many years of hard work out of him. *Hasta luego*, until then.'

I went indoors. Explained why Juan White Mule now had a brown one. We discussed the situation. Decided we would still refer to him as Juan White Mule. What would be the point in calling him Juan Brown Mule when there were so many Juans in the village, all with brown mules?

'A strange man,' I mused. 'He always told us, didn't he, that his mule was the best worker he ever had and that he would never part with it? The only mule in the whole village capable of pulling the plough on its own when he couldn't borrow a neighbour's to help? A strange man.'

Loli was Juan White Mule's youngest daughter; his three other children were all married and thriving. The eldest girl had married a businessman (where on earth had they met!). When he brought her and the three children to visit her parents, his big car caused quite a stir.

Juan's only son, at just over six foot, a good five inches taller than his father, was a fine strapping lad.

He obviously thought so, too. Even on chilly winter visits, he arrived clad only in shirt and jeans, the shirt open to the waist to display a chest thickly covered in black hair. As if this were not sight enough, he wore around his neck three gold chains with an assortment of trinkets attached, among which a shiny cross was prominent, as befitted a good if nominal Catholic.

Though he was scrupulously polite to us and found time to enquire after our health and family, I could not take to him. I suspected (quite wrongly, perhaps) that it was all put on to impress his dainty wife, who was not from the village – see how good friends *lawingléh* and my parents are, a prestigious fact.

The problem with Loli, Juan's youngest daughter, was who to get to marry her. She was already 25, slightly subnormal, threw her left foot as she walked and was formidably ugly, with a large mouth filled with mule-sized teeth.

She was, however, very well brought up by her mother, Maria, who belonged to the old school of village women with exquisite natural manners. Mannerly, pleasant and warm-hearted, Loli was a good cook and an excellent needlewoman. Her paellas, for instance, were as good as any I've eaten, and the embroidered linen and the crochet-work in her bottom drawer were as fine as any you'd find in the village.

Loli had one other great advantage. Her father was one of the largest landowners hereabouts. The land was split into smallish plots dotted over an area of about ten square kilometres, which is the usual way land is owned here. Her dowry, then, would be as good as any girl's, and better than most: a house (the bride's parents always provided the house) and enough land to make a living from.

Good negotiator as Juan was, no one in the village showed any interest in his offer, even though in this village, as elsewhere in the region, land marries land, often the most important consideration. So Loli at 25 was without a *novio*, a fiancé, while her friends of the same age were married and busy raising families.

Knowing Juan, we did not expect him to admit defeat. So we were not at all surprised one day to see him accompanied by a swarthy lean young man, who turned out to be Loli's *novio*. He was from Trevélez, the highest inhabited village in Europe, some hundred kilometres from our village up one of the most fiendishly steep, winding, narrow roads you could ever wish – or not wish – to drive.

The *novio*'s name was Rafael, the landless son of a mother widowed early after he was born. He was a peon, but there was never enough work on the scanty cultivable land around his village to keep him in constant employment.

The first thing I noticed about him was his long, loping, tireless stride. He leant forward, settled his weight over each foot as he put it down, then lifted himself to swing the next foot forward. He walked everywhere, he told me, often going 20 kilometres over the mountains to find work.

Juan knew – it was common knowledge – that the energy and stamina of the people who lived in the Sierra Nevada were phenomenal: he was as good a judge of man as mule. I realised at once he had got himself as good a worker as his white mule . . . And so it proved.

To prepare for the wedding, Juan, his wife and Loli moved out of their house while it was gutted and completely remade inside. This was the usual thing. All the relatives and friends invited to the wedding would meet at the house and be shown over it. If there was nothing new to see, Juan would lose face and his prestige would suffer.

Juan's house, two doors from ours, is set farther back into the hillside and reached by a steepish dirt path.

On the day of the wedding, about 60 people assembled in the house and on the patio to accompany bride and groom down through the village to the church. Much of the way was through the village streets, in reality unmade rutted paths. Rafael was dressed in a green suit, which fitted where it touched, red shoes and a violently purple striped shirt and tie, which he kept dragging at as if he were choking.

The men's *copas* were being filled with wine from half a dozen *garrafas*, 16 litres in each glass jar, from the best-known mountain bodega, El Casería. As the wine flowed, the chatter changed to shouting, each vainly trying to make himself heard above the din, the wives standing anxiously near.

Just as the church bell began to toll at five o'clock, Loli appeared in a long white hand-embroidered wedding dress, a fine mantilla of almost transparent lace, white stiletto-heeled shoes, and a bouquet of fragrant orange blossom, which all the women knew would bring the couple good luck. She was smiling, her eyes shining behind her large horn-rimmed glasses.

In the ear-splitting hubbub no one noticed the dark clouds that were scudding with increasing speed towards the village from the distant sierras. The very moment the procession, headed by bride and groom, left the house, it began to rain, a veritable cloudburst.

Juan, ever the man for any occasion, dashed indoors for an umbrella, which he held over Loli, whose tears were now flowing as freely as the raindrops were falling. The dirt path was now a streamlet. Loli lost her white satin shoes. Rafael picked them up, held them between thumb and forefinger away from his side as if he were afraid they would bite him.

By the time we got to the church, splashing through the mud, we were soaked to the skin. Only the bride and groom were silent. The rest chattered and shouted their way along, the men laughing unrestrainedly, all seemingly completely oblivious of the downpour.

The church seemed to us already full, but fortunately we were wrong. Ramón in his magnificent robes smilingly ushered us to the front. With much good-natured banter and pushing, we crammed into the long wooden, ornately-carved pews left vacant for us. Amid an incredible din of voices, young and old, the service proceeded at gratifying, not to say almost indecent, speed. For this we were more than grateful. The church, cold as a morgue at the best of times, was now glacial.

The best man fumbled for the ring – and the lights went out. I heard it tinkle sharply on the worn flagstones. Had it fallen down one of the cracks? If so, what would happen next? Poor Loli . . .

Padre Ramón and his acolytes were equal to the occasion. As if by magic, lighted candles appeared. The ring was found. Ramón, at an even brisker pace, brought the service to its conclusion.

The register signed, we emerged into brilliant blinding sunshine, the typical aftermath of such sudden storms, over as quickly as they come. We had missed the organ music, but nobody else had: there was no organ, nor had there ever been.

Loli and Rafael stood in front of the church door, Loli smiling ecstatically. Her mantilla was ruined; her orange-blossom bouquet had lost its fragrant petals; her long white dress was mud-stained and clung to her as if it had been poured on. (Why had I never noticed before what a splendid busty figure she had?)

Everyone came forward. Kissed the bride on both cheeks. Wished the newly married couple many happy years of life together. Thrust folded paper money into her waiting hands. This she passed to Rafael, who, smiling for the first time, stuffed it into the pockets of his grass-green suit.

The heat was now intense. By the time we arrived back at the house, we were more or less dried out.

The wedding feast, prepared by Loli's mother and her two sisters, was lavish. Paella, *morcilla*, blood sausage, *longaniza*, pork sausage, both these from their own pig killed two days before, salad with choice black olives, and mountain ham, the best *serrano* from Trevélez, a rare treat indeed, far too expensive for the villagers' pockets. The huge chunks of bread from the village bakery were still warm. Another treat; we all love *pan caliente*. Bread here, without butter or any other dressing except olive oil, is eaten at every meal – truly the staff of life.

Juan and his new son-in-law moved among the crowd, exhorting the men to help themselves from the half a dozen *garrafas*. I noted with satisfaction they needed no encouragement; the wine was already flowing like water. My neighbours saw to it that my glass was never empty. I am not fond of the mountain wine they drink in such quantities with every meal, but this – Juan had obviously paid a good price for this *clarete*, deep amber in colour and dry enough for my taste – was different.

The great virtue of mountain wine, so the villagers aver, is that it is made *sin química*, without chemicals. Most of it is in fact a *mosto*, a young wine, pure and untreated, meant to be drunk in the same year as the grapes are harvested. The men take pride in going to the mountain bodega of their choice and seeing their 16-litre *garrafas* filled from the huge oak barrels. They smile a little pityingly when they see my bottled wines – wine from a bottle with all its chemicals, never!

The El Casería wine I was drinking now, I had to admit, went very well with the superb food; and the more I drank, the better it tasted.

I looked around for Loli and Rafael; I wished to give them our best wishes once again. I asked Juan where were they. He smiled, shook his head. 'Gone, Alberto, on their *luna de miel*. If they had stayed any longer, our neighbours might think . . . Well, who knows what they might think?'

He asked me if I had seen over the new house. And Juanita? We hadn't. We followed Juan, and we in turn were followed by I don't know how many others, all pushing and scrambling to get the best view.

Did we like the new kitchen? We said we did, despite the fact the taps above the new sink were not connected and, as we knew full well, would never be.

Did we like the wallpaper in the little hall, the parlour, the two tiny bedrooms, each with a different pattern and differently coloured flowers, all the very latest? We said we did.

Did we like the *azulejos* on the floor, so much better than the old concrete. Of course we did, temporarily ignoring the fact that they and the wallpapers shouted at one another. But bright, though, very bright.

Juan paused dramatically before what we knew was the main bedroom. He flung open the double doors, turned triumphantly to us: 'What do you think of the bridal chamber?'

The whole room was decked out in crimson. Crimson tiles, crimson ceiling, crimson wallpaper. The dressing table had a crimson runner of intricate crochet-work, the toilet articles were crimson-backed.

The matrimonial bed was huge. Crimson coverlet, crimson headboard and satin hangings, even crimson pillows.

Juan was standing by the bedhead, looking at us expectantly. To be sure to be heard above the admiring murmurings of the onlookers, I said loudly: '*¡Estupendo, Juan amigo, todo estupendo!*'

This was exactly what Juan had been wanting: his neighbours and good friends, *lawingléh*, had proved he had such good taste, so what more was there to be said? Yet I could see he was

45

delighted also with the congratulations of the others present, especially those of the women.

We felt obliged to accept Loli's invitation to a meal, but did so with considerable foreboding.

The house Juan White Mule had provided his daughter and her husband with was at the village end of Calle Cruces, a little way up a steepish path and near the gypsy quarter. It had stood empty for some years. We had expected workmen to be busy about it putting it to rights in a frantic race against time before Loli and Rafael arrived back from their *luna de miel*, honeymoon. But no: all we saw were two gypsy women cleaning and lime-washing outside and in. We were all the more astonished, because we were well aware of how quickly these cob-walled and reed-roofed houses deteriorated without constant attention.

We arrived at 2.15, thinking this was just about right; families here eat their *almuerzo*, their main meal, anytime between two and four.

We exchanged kisses, Loli's real kisses instead of the normal token, and she uttered the traditional greeting: 'Be at home here. My house is your house.'

I asked where Rafael was.

'In the *vega* working, of course!' Loli cried, her tone clearly implying this was the only possible place he could be. 'But he knows you're coming. He will not forget. He will be here soon . . . Sit down, sit down, please.'

The living room was like a cave and just as cold. A trestle-table and four wooden rush-seated chairs with tall and very upright backs were all the furniture, except for a big battered calor-gas stove.

Loli went into the kitchen. We followed her in, drawn by the sight of the fire blazing on the hearth.

The kitchen was very small. The sink was badly cracked and I wondered whether the tap above it was connected. The paella was already beginning to sizzle in its enormous blackened iron pan, which I recognised as Loli's mother's, balanced precariously on a small trivet.

I stretched out my hands to the blaze, breathed deeply, the smell of the woodsmoke blending with that of the paella. '¡*Que aroma buena!*' I said. 'We will stand by the fire for a while.'

'Of course. As you wish.'

Loli divided her time between the paella and preparing a big salad on the trestle-table. Her crockery and kitchen utensils, we saw, were in boxes against one wall.

After 20 minutes or so, Loli lifted the paella off the fire and placed it on the hearth. 'Rafael will not forget,' she kept periodically reassuring us. 'He is coming soon.'

It was close to 3.30 when Rafael arrived. In one hand he had a bunch of spring onions, a sign, perhaps, he had not forgotten. Tired, hungry, he greeted us without warmth and told us to come and eat.

Loli dumped down a plate with a tablespoon and fork on it and a napkin of fine linen, with L R embroidered in the corner.

'Glasses, woman,' Rafael said. He could hardly wait for them to be produced before filling them with what I judged from its colour was *clarete* left over from the wedding feast.

'*Salud*,' he said, but instead of draining his glass, as I expected, he only sipped the wine.

Loli brought in the sizzling paella, supporting its weight as best she could. Rafael placed a folded grain sack in the middle of the table and Loli was glad to rest the heavy pan on it.

When she had fetched the salad and the six *barillas*, small bars of fresh bread, she looked at Rafael before she sat down.

'Water, woman, water,' he said. 'Who can quench his thirst with wine?'

Rafael pointed to the five-litre *garrafa* his wife was bringing in. 'From La Patrona, the patron saint of the village. Pure water.'

No one in the village except ourselves drank tap water. Too full of lime, they believed, and this gave you kidney stones, whereas water from La Patrona, the village fountain, contained many trace elements necessary for good health. When I suggested it also must contain many microbes, I was always shouted down.

And another thing. You could not cook with tap water. The *garbanzos*, for instance, to try and eat these chickpeas cooked in tap water was to break your teeth. Tapwater was for washing.

'Eat, eat,' Loli said as she sat down.

We waited until Rafael had filled his plate before we helped ourselves. We were by now very hungry, but this paella would have tasted just as delicious under any circumstances. The saffron-coloured rice was laden with mussels, small clams and prawns, chicken pieces, rabbit pieces, slices of black pudding and sausage, only the mussels, prawns and clams being bought from the fish man that morning, all garnished with olives and red and black peppers.

Though Loli drank nothing, she ate as heartily as her husband. We had eaten our fill, were very content to sit and watch the two of them not stop till only a little rice remained in the huge pan.

Neither of them had used their napkins, as we had done, I with great pleasure: I heartily dislike the paper napkins increasingly used in café-bars and bar-restaurants nowadays.

At last our hosts finished eating, Rafael sighing with satisfaction and reflectively rubbing his full stomach. We took care to thank them, though knowing full well it was not expected. I crowned the thanks by telling Loli it was as good a paella as her mother could cook.

And now, I thought, for the big moment.

Loli seemed to read my thoughts. 'You have not seen our bedroom. Come.'

How, I thought, would the bridal suite look in such a room as the one we had just eaten in?

The only article in the whitewashed, cement-floored bedroom was an old iron double bed. The multicoloured patchwork quilt was undoubtedly Loli's own work.

What on earth were we to say?

I struggled. 'This room. Too small . . . *La cama matrimonio*, the bridal bed, even on its own would be too big . . .'

It became clear that, if we were embarrassed, they were not.

My curiosity got the better of me. Had they ever slept in that magnificent bridal bed? Yes, they had. For a week after returning from their *luna de miel* before moving into their present house. It was in the matrimonial bed, they felt sure, that Loli became pregnant.

And who was using the bridal bedroom now? No one. Why ever not? Juan and his wife would not feel comfortable there. And what was going to happen to all the furniture, including, of course, the magnificent bed?

It was Rafael, shrugging his shoulders, who answered: 'It will remain where it is. Perhaps when we have a bigger house, Juan will decide I have worked long enough to earn the bed and all the furniture . . . but it's not important. Here we have a roof over our head and food enough to eat. What more can a married couple want with a child on the way?'

He thought a moment longer. 'And land. The land is my woman's. She has the deeds. Her father cannot take that back. So . . .' He smiled, shrugged again. 'We are happy. I have work to do. Every day, not just some days as it was with me in Trevélez. I want no more.'

This question of land. How wise, I reflected, that the wife keeps possession of the land she brings into the marriage. She is undisputed mistress of the house, true; what she says, goes. This, husbands freely and cheerfully acknowledge to me as man to man: '*Hombre*, is it not the same everywhere?' But her status and power is firmly founded on the fact she is a landowner in her own right. Would not a husband think long and hard before jettisoning both wife and land?

And children. A married couple have a child as soon as possible. The nuclear family can then become part of the extended family. These villagers have no concept of friendship as we understand it. What counts with them is *la familia*, and only *la familia*. If members of the extended family fall out, as they do sometimes, and then so bitterly that they no longer have anything whatsoever to do with each other, it is always over land.

For the husband, another advantage of putting his wife in the family way is that she is thereby well and truly tied to the house, her freedom of movement strictly curtailed. And living next door or close to other members of the extended family, as is their custom – parents, brothers, sisters, cousins – he need never worry about his wife's virtue.

Everyone here seems genuinely fond of children. Fathers dote on their offspring as much as mothers, spoil them just as outrageously. Boys in particular; boys are expected to get their own way, proof they are *muy macho*. Who, they ask rhetorically, would want a son to grow up to be a *maricón*, a nancy boy?

Yet, to our perpetual amazement, these wilfully spoiled children turn into such admirable adolescents and adults.

Loli and Rafael named their daughter Rosita. A dainty, attractive baby, she grew into a bright-eyed, equally attractive child. At the age of three, she had a most loving nature, a ready tongue, and was obviously bright as the proverbial button.

Soon after, she went to live with her aunt, Juan White Mule's eldest daughter. 'Much better for her,' Juan assured me. 'She will go to a good school, she will need education in the future, and she will have many advantages that Loli cannot provide for her.'

Rosita did return most weekends. She stayed with her grandparents and only spent a little time with her parents.

By now, Loli had another daughter; this time, alas, so handicapped that she was to remain a baby, unable to do anything for herself, to walk, or even to utter an intelligible word. Growing, yes, but the extra apparently boneless bulk only making her more difficult to cope with. She spent long periods in hospital, but only, in our opinion, to be experimented on, for she made no progress whatsoever.

Little wonder that the simple-minded Loli began to deteriorate. Lost her good manners, her good nature. Became louder, coarser, untidier in dress and appearance – not helped, either, by living in the same house under the same conditions as when we had our first and only meal there.

There was no money to spare, or so it seemed. Was this, I wondered, because, as his wife's land was not enough to keep them, Rafael was forced to work some of his father-in-law's land and Juan was only paying him a peon's wage, not the half-share in all that was produced, as was normal when land was rented?

From time to time I enquired – but only from Juan himself – how Baby Emilia was, to be met with a dismissive shrug and a placid smile: 'No better. Never will be. God's will. *¿Qué vamos a hacer? ¿Es la vida, verdad?* What can we do? That's life, isn't it?'

5

Paco, the village baker, 'he from Berja', is enormously fat, stands in his bakehouse panting, sweating, watching with satisfaction the fire's golden mouth devour the wood he is feeding it.

'*Hombre!* Any bread not baked in the oven over a fire of *leña*, wood, is not bread as we knew it of old in Berja. Now, where is such a procedure – the old true way – to be found? Nowhere except here. And the flour they use. All the goodness taken out of it. White as a virgin's face when she goes the first time to the *cama matrimonio*. Flour? White graveyard dust . . . Not like my flour, grey, the colour flour should be, milled between stones, nothing robbed from it.'

Paco pauses to wipe the sweat from his face and arms. He glances at us to make sure he has our full attention, then lifts his huge cupped hands to his mouth, blows hard, making a hissing sound.

'Like balloons, their bread. Light. Filled with air. Worthless. More air than flour.'

He opens the oven door, reveals row on row of loaves – *barras*, *roscas*, rings, big and small round ones – dumbly baking in the red heat, the low brick arched roof above.

'Nearly done.' Paco smiles, wipes the sweat from his huge swarthy face, his black hair glistening.

The waiting women grouped behind him fall silent as they smell the cherished fragrance. Soon now they will hurry home with the rings, hot from the glowing oven, tucked in their linen bags, to break and eat with their children before it cools. Never was such tasty bread as this, so crusty, smelling so good: little wonder that *pan caliente*, warm bread, is such a universal favourite.

Only one man disagrees with this view. A little white-haired man, a perpetually sour expression on his lean pointed-chinned face, he was born and bred in the village. When he married, he moved to the nearby town. Recently widowed, he has come back to the village to live with his long-suffering daughter. Nothing in the village satisfies him, least of all the baker.

This little man buttonholes me whenever he can. After the usual greeting and the enquiry after my *mujer*, woman, and family, he turns at once to his favourite theme, holding me by the elbow.

'That Paco, he of Berja, he uses third-class flour. Grey as dust. The controlled price of bread means that he of Berja grows even fatter by the day on the profits he makes . . . And we, we have to eat this bread. It lies on my stomach like a stone. Why can't he buy decent white flour to make bread like I've been eating all these years? It is a disgrace. And nobody but the people here would put up with it, they know no better.'

Now, whenever we see Third-Class Flour coming, we do our very best to avoid him.

Paco's wife, Dolores, is small, buxom, pert and quick as a Spanish sparrow. Like her husband, she still speaks with a Berja accent, much easier to understand than the village dialect.

Chicharrones are small pieces of pork crackling. During the pig-killing season, the great treat is to bring your crackling to the bakehouse. Dolores – this is Dolores's job – will bake for you a flat dough cake, the *chicharrones* mixed with sultanas. You wait for it to come out of the oven, then rush home to share the hot pieces with your family, a rare treat.

If you have no crackling, then you cannot have any *chicharrones* cake, for you cannot buy it.

Paco is an avid Western reader. Between the four, sometimes five, batches of bread he bakes each day, you will often find him sitting in the heat of the bakery reading a Western. Not the kind we're used to, but small-format, simply written paperbacks of anything up to 50 pages long.

I used to buy a few from time to time and give them to him: it genuinely pleased him to receive, and it pleased me to give.

Imagine our surprise when one evening shortly after the pig-

53

killing season had begun in December, Dolores arrived at our *casa* with a flat tin covered over with a cloth.

'*Pase, pase*, come in, Dolores,' I said, genuinely pleased to see her bright little face.

'No, Alberto, *gracias, no tengo tiempo*', thank you, I haven't time.

Before I could protest, she handed me the warm tin.

'A *regalito* for Juanita. If it gets cold, heat it up in the oven.'

Before I could thank her, she was gone.

The *regalito*, the little present, was a big slab of *chicarrones*, enough to last us at least a week; it's too fatty to eat much at a sitting.

'I wonder,' I said as we hastily sat down to eat a piece while it was still warm, 'if this isn't a return for the little paperbacks I've given to Paco?'

'I shouldn't be surprised.' Joan nodded. 'Quite probably. We know full well you can't give them anything unless they give you something back.'

Right or wrong, every year from then on until Paco died of a heart attack, Dolores brought Joan her *regalito*.

Paco and his wife were strangers when they came from Berja 20 years ago, having brought their bread daily from Berja on the back of two mules down that steep winding mountain road, a feat to be wondered at, and strangers they still are. This they know, and shrug it off with a smile. Their opinion of the villagers, often expressed to us by Dolores (in strict confidence, of course) is that they are, as everyone else who doesn't live in the village admits, *una gente muy rara*, a very peculiar kind of people. Dolores and her husband have long ago given up any attempt to understand them. The sparkle in Dolores's eyes as she says this, the half-hidden contemptuous smile on her plump lips, tell us plainly that she is enjoying paying them back to her *caros amigos* Alberto y Juanita.

If you walk into the mouth of any of our nearby *arroyos*, narrow gorges as often dry as not, you will notice that many of those ancient almond trees planted by the Moors all those long centuries ago and no longer capable of bearing a worthwhile crop have been cut down. This is chiefly the work of Paco and the *gitanos*. Heating an oven with a wood fire is all very well, but where is the steady supply of wood to come from?

Paco's little donkey's coat, like its master's hair, is black as the almonds' trunks. The sideless cart seems much too big for the donkey to pull. To see it piled with *leña*, the huge Paco perched at the front, the willing little donkey straining between the shafts, is one of our most treasured sights.

Often, when they have been some distance in the intense heat of the sun, the little donkey's coat is as plastered to its skin as is Paco's thick black hair.

Paco never passes us without stopping for a chat. 'This *leña*,' he solemnly assures us, 'belongs to nobody. When it does, I get permission to take it.'

We find his anxiety touching – as if we cared how he came by the precious wood.

To see this great man wielding the axe behind the bakehouse, chopping the wood into the required size, the splinters flying, is another treasured sight.

Once I ventured, when he paused to catch his breath, 'But your little donkey . . . ?'

There was no need to finish my question; he took my meaning at once.

'This *burro*? Young and strong. He pulls well. But when we come to a slope, I get down and help him pull. No need to worry, don Alberto. I feed him as well as I feed my own family. Think, for instance, of all yesterday's bread I put into his manger, a good use for it. Nobody here wants yesterday's bread, it's *pan tierno*, today's bread, for them, as you well know.'

The sharp dry sound of an axe from the deep ravine below us shatters a silence redolent of sage, gorse and rosemary. A *gitano*, brown mule by his side, saddlecloth bright as fresh blood, is hacking down an almond tree in the stifling sun of early afternoon.

He has seen us, although he has not raised his head or paused in his chopping. He knows us, knows, too, we will not interfere. Nobody will be out in this sun. The villagers will all be having their siesta, good reason for him to be at work . . .

We watch him cut through the trunk and lop the arthritic branches before splitting it. He carefully adds what he has cut to the two neat piles, wraps cord around each, uses all his lean weight to tighten and knot the cord, then lifts each pile and settles it into one of the twin big woven panniers on either side of the mule.

Satisfied, he looks up. I lift my hand, and he acknowledges my greeting with a nod. He turns and begins to walk down the dry river bed, the mule close at heel. Soon he will be back home in his *barrio*, where in front of her door in the shade of the rudimentary porch made of *cañas*, reeds, and plastic his *mujer* is waiting to cook the meal. Who in their senses will pay for a *bombona* of *butano*, the big yellow bottles of gas delivered monthly to the village and which we all use for our cooking, when there is *leña* to be had for the fetching?

I gaze at the numerous black sentinel almonds that still stand guard up the ravine, each sharply defined in the clear air. Twelve centuries ago the conquering Moors planted them, directed their slaves to set in place the supporting stones that held the pockets of precious earth in which the trees were to grow and flourish, and I wondered again at the knowledge of the race so despised by my neighbours. But then, if your forebears had been slaves . . .

For me standing here in this instant of unbroken silence, it is as if that solitary *gitano*, Moors' pure blood in his dark veins, innocent as the axe he wields, has severed the blackened trunk of time itself from its roots.

6

The Jiménez family lives three doors down from us.

Grandfather Pedro is in his mid-eighties. We call him *El Bicicletista* because he is never seen away from the house without his ancient bicycle.

Over the rough village roads it is much better support than a walking stick. 'And how could I go to town all those kilometres away once every fortnight on market day if I could not ride my bicycle?'

'But your sons could take you in the mule cart.'

'My sons? Who would want to depend on his sons for everything? To be treated as an old man?'

This was as far as his independence went. On his eightieth birthday his daughter, Maria, moved into his little house next door to his two sons' houses to cook and do for him.

'We are good company for each other,' he told me. 'She is mistress here in her own house, for that is what it will be after I am dead.' He paused a moment as if to digest this inevitability. 'What is an unmarried girl worth in her brother's house? Nothing, as you well know. Except to do what everybody tells her – sons, their women, the children. True, she still gets out of the house to go three half-days a week to the canning factory – you have seen the bus collecting the girls from the *plaza* – but that is no work for a girl born and bred in my village. My daughter – my daughter should be married. At work in the fields with her husband. Giving him children. Mistress in her own house.' He sighed deeply.

I did not dare ask why she was not married, but he interpreted my look correctly.

'When she was in flower, she was pretty. She would draw a man to her . . .'

He gazed at me without seeing me.

'But she is still pretty. A fine figure of a woman.' I was not flattering him. I had always been curious why a woman blessed with such looks had never married.

'Now?' He grimaced. 'Now she is old. Far too old for anybody to want to marry her. She has missed her chance. Why? She did not wish to marry. My sons and I would have provided the dowry. We have land enough.' He sighed again. 'I pleaded with her. I brought suitable young men to the house. Good sons of good friends of mine. She refused them all. Why? She did not wish to marry. Too proud. Nobody was good enough for her.'

I saw how desolate he was looking and mumbled something about marriage not being the only life for a girl nowadays – an idiotic statement in this context. Fortunately he did not seem to hear me.

'And now? What is there ahead of her? To be a spinster. Mocked behind her back. To grow old alone. No children to look after her in her old age. That is not the fate I would wish for any daughter of mine.'

Village girls in flower strolling arm in arm. They chatter, noisy and vivid as parrots. Unflawed skin, brilliant eyes, milky teeth, their skirts swirl as they make their animated way along the path. How quickly the flower fades in the heat of the south.

At the village dance, the girls wait, gaze almost without breathing at the knots of boys against the far wall. The lads are shy, eyes fixed fascinated in a sweet dream on the girls in perfect flower. How quickly the flower fades in the heat of the South.

At the wedding, the happy garrulous crowd endlessly toasting the bride and groom in pink mountain wine. The bride, delicate and fragrant as the orange blossom she wears, a girl in perfect flower. How quickly the flower fades in the heat of the South.

Rosa Sol is Pedro's granddaughter. Her mother, Rosario, tall, slim, still with a winning girlish air, has the most magnificent pair of breasts you could ever wish to see, unsurpassable in the village. We were not at all surprised when her husband announced soon after we settled in that Rosario had given birth to their son exactly nine months to the day after they were married. Moreover, if that were not matter enough for pride, their daughter, Rosa Sol, followed only ten months later.

'Poor Rosario,' I said, keeping a straight face, 'have you no shame?'

He glanced fleetingly at Joan before he answered. '*Hombre!* Shame? Shame? Don't you know yet the blood runs faster here? My woman is as proud as I am. Look at our two. Could anybody have finer children?'

We had to agree they could not. Anyone would be pleased to have such children.

Rosa Sol was now 19. What pleasure we took in watching from our *terraza* as she and her three friends passed our door on their noisy way to Sunday six o'clock evening mass; their perfume floated up to us as they waved and called their greeting. Happy girls in perfect flower – and we were happy for them.

Rosa Sol was a smaller replica of her mother, as girlishly shy and winsome in manner, as attractive in looks. Small-breasted, though, but prettily so.

Soon we learned that her three friends had *novios*, fiancés. 'And Rosa?' I asked her mother. 'Has Rosa a *novio*?'

'No. She does not seem interested.' Rosario smiled, somewhat ruefully. 'There is still time. True?'

I said there was plenty of time. After all, she was still only 19.

I began to tease Rosa Sol. When was she going to have a *novio* like her friends? She would blush a little, toss her head, smile and reply: 'Nobody has come forward yet.'

I soon gave up teasing her. I saw it made her uncomfortable. This I did not want; I was by now very fond of her. Was she, I asked myself, going to follow in her aunt's footsteps? If so, why? I hardly dared ask myself. In this macho society they admit there are homosexuals, but lesbians – impossible!

The name of Rosa Sol's dog is Ofelia. Rather a grand name for a little smooth-haired terrier, white with four black paws, but then she was Spanish. She likes to be petted, and we like to pet her. She wriggles with pleasure, her tail seeming to be the motive power.

When we are cooking pork or chicken for supper, she scratches at the door. I open the upper half, tell her to come back in the morning for the bones. She invariably does.

One morning, as soon as she saw us leave the house, she rushed up to us. Began to bark and jump up at us, a thing she had never done before. Then she scurried off towards her house, came back and repeated the performance.

We were completely baffled. What on earth was she trying to tell us? We did notice, however, that each time she ran a little way farther . . .

Suddenly it dawned on us: she wanted us to follow her.

As soon as we began to move forward, Ofelia became even more excited. Barked louder. Dashed to and fro even more frenziedly until we were almost level with her house. Then she sprinted to the corral next to the house and jumped up and over the half-door.

We hurried to the door and looked in. The first thing we saw was the two goats patiently waiting to be led out to pasture, one of Rosa Sol's jobs. Hens and chicks were scratching about in the litter.

In the far corner was Ofelia. Lying on her side on the clean straw, she was manoeuvring the fat brown puppy towards her so that it could suckle, her eyes fixed on us.

We went in and made a great fuss of her and the puppy. We knew it was her first. That she wanted so desperately for us to share her triumph was something we shall never forget.

The old man we call Manolo Nicho because he looks after the niches in the cemetery came to put down the rat poison.

'Is it necessary?' I asked him. 'The rats are kept well under control by the cats and dogs. Proof – I have never seen a rat.'

Manolo rubbed the white stubble on his chin. His look told

me that only someone not born and bred in the village would ask such a fool question.

'Who am I to ask if it is necessary? It is the *ayuntamiento*, town council, who employs me once a year to put down the bait. I obey my orders . . . Cats! I know nothing about cats. And you, Alberto, you are fortunate. You have no corral. No need of one. No pigs, goats, rabbits, hens, so no rats. You do not even see one.'

'But each man can deal with the rats in his own corral, surely?'

'Who knows? Some do not even notice them. They live in peace together. The rats breed and grow fat. And at night, when you are asleep, Alberto, they come out. That is when they take my bait out here and die.' He spat, wiped the saliva from his lips with the back of his hand. 'And good riddance, say I.'

'But the cats, the dogs. They also may take the bait and die. A horrible death. Good riddance to them also, you think?'

Manolo shook his head in despair. 'Cats? What are cats? What do cats matter? As for dogs, each man must look after his own.' He shrugged dismissively. 'There are too many stray dogs coming into the village these days. Once their owners would have shot them when they no longer wanted them. Now it is not worth the price of a cartridge, so they turn them away. Too many hungry dogs also that belong to the village. Their owners no longer bother to feed them. It is only those dogs, the strays and the hungry, that will take the bait. I know.'

'I still think there is a risk. It is dangerous. I —'

'You have a complaint, Alberto? Then make it to the Sanitation. They may listen to *you*. *Adios*.'

Manolo turned his back on me, resumed his methodical pacing, stopping at regular intervals to lay the bait.

I had not admitted even to myself that my chief fear about the rat poison was that Ofelia would be tempted to take it. Though Rosa Sol fed her well, she seemed always hungry when she waited outside our door for the bones.

Alas, my fear was well founded. Two mornings later, there was no Ofelia waiting at our door. I went down to Rosa Sol's house. She herself answered my call. Yes, Ofelia was dead. The rat poison.

61

'Poor Ofelia. I *am* sorry, Rosa Sol. Truly sorry. I shall miss her.'

Rosa Sol smiled brightly. 'So shall I. But what can we do? That's life, isn't it?'

I knew how genuinely fond of Ofelia she was. Why, then, did she not appear the least bit sad?

Then I remembered the deep streak of fatalism the villagers, in common with other Andalusians, have inherited from the Moors, which was how the Muslim Arabs who surged out of the Middle East in the seventh century into North Africa and then across the Straits of Gibraltar in 711 to conquer Spain and rule it for almost 800 years, were known, though they themselves never used the term.

Over the years we were to meet this ingrained fatalism again and again ... A disaster? A death of someone in the family, even? You accepted it without complaint, using the standard form of words Rosa Sol had used:

¿Qué vamos a hacer? ¿Es la vida, verdad? What can we do? That's life, isn't it?

Most, if not all, Andalusians have Moorish blood in their veins. Some, judging by their looks — very swarthy skin, hawk nose, dark-brown almond-shape eyes — are still pure Moor, or at least more Moor than Spaniard.

The myth still persists here in the village, as elsewhere in Andalusia, that the Moorish occupation was a complete disaster. The Moors were the enemy; the expulsion of the Moors after their almost eight centuries of domination, an unmitigated blessing. It was a holy Catholic war against these Muslim Arabs, and one that was won with God's help.

The truth was the exact opposite. The expulsion of the Moors and Jews in the fifteenth century plunged Spain into a cultural night from which they have only recently been emerging. With their departure went Spain's world leadership in music, literature, philosophy, architecture, mathematics and science. Córdoba, for instance, in its heyday had half a million inhabitants and was rivalled only by Constantinople and Baghdad. How appropriately ironic that after the reconquest Córdoba's magnificent mosque should be desecrated by building a Catholic church in its centre.

It is only comparatively recently that Spaniards have brought themselves to take cognizance of their Islamic past. Their pride in their *sangre pura*, their pure blood, was shattered when they had to acknowledge that there was no such thing: who could truly claim there was no Moorish blood in the veins of their ancestors?

This enlightenment has not yet penetrated our village. Here they still despise, if not actually hate, the *Moros*. Strange, indeed, when they know (surely?) that the irrigation system without which nothing would grow in our valley, let alone the three crops a year they now harvest, was laid down by the Moors and has remained unchanged to this day. True, many of the *acequias*, the water channels, have had their original stone walls replaced by cement or pipes, but their position and direction is the same as it always was.

To call someone a Moor is an insult. I remember Pepe, one of the two bootblacks in the nearby fishing port – the other one is a deaf mute – complaining bitterly to me that people jeered at his son because he was a Moor.

'He is not,' he cried, 'we are not Moors, any more than they are!'

I looked at his son standing quietly at his side. I could see why he was so called: unless appearances lied, he was certainly a Moor, and a pure-blooded one at that.

Ironically, just as the Aussies have bought up and colonised much of England – the Convicts' Revenge! – so the Moors have come back to Granada. These Arabs have used their petrodollars to buy many of the *cármenes*, the lovely houses in the Albaicín, the old district, to live where once their ancestors lived.

These houses, shut off by high walls, have pleasant gardens surrounding a patio where fountains play. From their viewing towers, you can contemplate the grey sierras, the green *vega*, the russet Alhambra, your neighbours' tiled roofs.

Little wonder the Granada poet Soto de Rojas in the seventeenth century described the *cármenes* as 'a paradise barred to the majority, a garden available to the few'.

According to a young student friend of mine, these 'Moors' stalk about a city which was once entirely theirs as if it were so again; the one who owns what was once de Falla's is simply bursting with arrogance.

As for the Granada University professors, some of the old ones still declare openly the Falangists were right to have executed Federico García Lorca, that Red, that *maricón*, pitiable pansy.

'Can you wonder, Alberto,' Vitor said, righteous anger overcoming his sad sense of loss, 'we students know that democracy is coming *poco a poco*, little by little, if it is coming at all?'

7

The old men when they retire never do another hand's stroke: who would want to after a hard life spent working in the fields seven days a week? Holidays? What are holidays? The land cannot wait while you have a holiday.

In winter they spend their time sitting in the sun chatting with friends who are also *jubilado* – the lovely Spanish word for 'retired', suggesting as it does to us unending joy.

They also frequent the bars to play dominoes and cards, using pebbles, spent matches and bottle tops to bet with. If they buy a drink, which is rare, it is a *café solo*, a small black coffee, or a *chato de vino*, a small glass of mountain wine.

They go home only to sleep and eat; the house is the woman's domain, no place for a man.

They live as they have always lived – by the sun, not the clock. Their naked light bulbs (shades are unknown) are of the lowest possible wattage: who would willingly pay for electricity you do not need? The light is quite adequate to eat their supper by and go to bed. They do not read, not even the few who can. Their world is the village and the *vega*. They mind their own business, keep their head down, a habit that ensured they survived during Franco's 40-year dictatorship, a habit they find difficult if not impossible to shake off.

They do not usually live to a great age, as do many of the women. Their sole purpose in life, it seems, was to work. *Hay que trabajar*, we must work, they tell you on every occasion. And when I teasingly ask them why, why must they always be working, they have no answer.

Their days are also shortened, I believe, by the fact that once they stop work they take no exercise whatsoever: even walking is anathema.

Their wives, on the contrary, follow the same routine as before. Do the housework. Meet and chat with their neighbours when they go shopping. Cook the same meals at the same time – their men's appetites do not lessen. Look after their grand-children, many of whom they bring up, their mothers being at full stretch working in the fields side by side with their husbands.

Though they put on their *luto*, their mourning clothes, when their husbands die, and never wear another coloured garment, they seem to enjoy life, perhaps more than before.

There are exceptions. These 'Crying Graces', except to go to mass, never leave the house unless they have to, relying on their daughters or other members of the family to do their shopping. On the (fortunately) rare occasions I bump into them, common decency forces me to ask how they are.

The tears immediately begin to flow and I am regaled with the same tale as before. The unparalleled virtues of the departed husband are listed, and I am informed of how the widow cannot wait to join him, so-and-so that he really was.

Their family show them infinite patience, consideration and respect. They visit them daily, often providing their main meal.

Only their neighbours seem to have some reservations, cau-tiously expressed by the familiar *¿Qué vamos a hacer?* followed by the hope the widow may soon be allowed to join her man in heaven, though the words they use to express this concept are *el cielo*, the sky, *la gloria* or *el paraíso*.

Not all the men retire as soon as they get their pension. Nico is one such.

'Retire, Alberto? Not me. What life is it to sit all day doing nothing? Telling your neighbours what they already know. How hard you worked. How much land you had. How fortunate your children are, especially the husbands of your daughters, to inherit such land. To spend all your days in idleness. No, Alberto, I will retire when death takes me. We prefer to work, my woman and I. Going to the market every fortnight. Meeting people we know. Sharing a glass with them.'

'And a coffee for Ana, I hope,' I add, knowing perfectly well what his answer will be.

'Ana? No, Alberto. *Mi mujer* drinks only water. She waits for me outside the bars without complaining. There are always women passing for her to chat to.'

Weighed down with age, well wrapped up, Pepe sits outside his door on a small wooden chair in the winter sun.

He is weaving stems of esparto grass into a string that nobody will ever use. When he stops and lifts his head, he gazes out over the *vega*.

He begins his weaving again, and now he is muttering to himself, but too indistinctly for me to make out what. He lifts his head again as I approach to greet him. Although I think he no longer sees well enough to tell for certain one man from another, he recognises my voice.

'Pepe, friend, how are you?'

'Alberto, isn't it? Well, how should I be? I am here, there's no more to be said. And waiting, Alberto, waiting.'

He makes a vague gesture across the *vega* at the cemetery.

Pepe's devoted wife died only last year. Although his faithful daughter comes every day to feed and look after him, I've no need to ask Pepe what he is waiting for.

We recognise the old man from the *cortijo*; he is the one who killed Gafas.

His mountain mule is almost as tall as a horse, its harness bright as beaded curtains, the long tassels of the saddle-cloth a bright scarlet.

He sits astride his stirrupless saddle that looks like a mattress securely cinched. His velvet suit is autumn-coloured, his low-crowned, wide-brimmed hat, black. His neckerchief echoes the colour of the saddle-cloth tassels.

His wife, black shawl clutched around her shoulders, dressed all in black, flattens herself against her husband's back.

We look at the huge plaited panniers and see the rosy, well-scrubbed feet of a pig protruding from each.

The only sound is the soft falling of the mule's careful hooves on the dust of the narrow path. It seems to be dozing, yet its long slack ears point the way unfailingly.

The early morning sun brightens, warms the old pair and their hope of a good price. They smile at us as they pass.

'A good price, I hope,' I call.

'A good day, two good pigs, so there will be a good price,' the old man replies, and both smile again.

There is only one unmarried woman who works her own land. When she was young, she wore a pistol at her hip. This, they tell me, was because she was very desirable, and who knows what could happen to a woman working on her own on her *parcelas*? *Una mujer muy valiente*, very courageous, *valiente*, being a word they reserve for someone they really admire.

When I first met Elena, she was weather-beaten, wrinkled, lean, old before her time. However late she returned from the fields, she always reined in her tiny donkey whenever she met me to enquire after my woman and my family.

No one uses her name: she is *la soltera*, the spinster, and when the men say the word, there is always a note of pity in their voice.

When I got to know Elena well, I questioned her about her life, assuring her I had heard about her early days and how much I admired her courage.

'Well, yes, Alberto, it's been a hard life. I own little *parcelas* in various places. There on the edge of the village, I work two, *muy conveniente*. But I've five more farther away up the valley on both sides of the river. I work them all without help, I cannot afford to hire a peon. And at the end of each long hard day, I go home to an empty house. Dark enough, except when I bring some carnations indoors and put them in a jar on the table.'

'Your little donkey,' I said in an effort to cheer her up a bit, 'he reminds me of the most famous donkey in Spain. He was called Platero, and –'

'I know no Platero.' Elena did not smile.

'Well, anyway,' I said, 'your little donkey is the same colour, moon-silver and steel.'

At Elena's complete look of incomprehension, I felt a bigger fool than ever. I desperately tried to rescue the conversation.

'And what is your little *burro* called?'

'It's not a *burro*, it's a *burra* . . . It has no name. *Burra* is enough, don't you think? But I love my donkey.'

In the pause that followed, I could think of nothing else to say. I need not have worried; *la soltera* was pursuing her own train of thought.

'I love my *burra*. If someone had loved me when I was young, how different my life would have been. But happier? Who knows? Only *El Señor*, not I.'

Elena's elder sister, Maria, a large, black-haired, big-busted widow, lives in Calle Cruces, a few doors from us. Either by choice or necessity, she is the only one who did not have a W C installed when her neighbours did. Every morning she emerges, in one hand her ancient pail, in the other, her trowel, to cross the road and bury her night-soil under the prickly pears. Yet even before this universal practice died out, there was never any smell. The expert burying and the dry climate? We don't know. What we do know, however, is how glad we were of this fact. Maria was the only one in our *barrio*, quarter, who did not have a W C installed.

Next door to her is her corral, now no longer in use. On her clothes line in front of it regularly appear tiny black silk pants with intricate lace where it matters most.

I find these pants even more fascinating when I think of the one who wears them. What, I ask myself, impels this great woman, now in her late fifties, to wear such a garment? Can it possibly be that, as she daily steps into them – or more tellingly out of them! – they recall torrid nights of past passion? Forbidden visions that . . .

I often question my wife. She has little to add to my entranced musings, is in reality as baffled as I.

When I missed Elena and her gallant little donkey, I asked Maria Passion-Pants what had happened. In her sing-song voice and carefully articulated Spanish she told me sadly that her sister last week had a stroke. Very severe. She was now helpless, unable to speak or move.

Truly shaken, I expressed my sympathy and offered my sincerest good wishes for her speedy and complete recovery. To be met with moist eyes, a resigned shrug, and '*¿Qué vamos a hacer? ¿Es la vida, verdad? La voluntad de Dios.*'

Elena, alas, made only a partial recovery. She now lives with her brothers; they take it in turns to look after her and work her land between them.

When I ask Maria, as I sometimes do, how her sister is, there is impatience mixed with disdain in her reply: 'Lena, Lena is a child again. Does nothing but eat. You would not know her, she who was so thin. She has become so fat the problem now is how to look after her, move her and clean her. My sister-in-laws have husbands and children of their own to care for. They will soon be worn out. What will become of them? As for Lena, Lena has no conscience, thinks only of herself and her food. There is no satisfying her. A greedy child. What is to become of them all? What are they to do with Lena? That I do not know. What I do know is that I cannot have her here. My house is too small, I could not lift her, and I have money enough only for my own needs.'

8

Patricio, Isabel and their daughters, Isabelita and Mari Puri, short for 'Purificatión', are our next-door neighbours. Isabel was born and bred in a village high up in the sierras, and it was there Patricio had to go to be married, the marriage having been arranged by their parents, though where and when I never found out. What I do know is that Patricio's father provided the house, a big one with five bedrooms and two corrals, one for the mule and hens, the other for the pigs, contrary to the established custom here of the bride's parents giving the house.

Our first invitation was from our neighbours to a picnic. Both our autosleeper and Patricio's ancient *furgoneta*, recently acquired 'new second-hand', one of the first in the village, were crammed with *familia*, mostly young girl cousins, and we set off up the tortuous steep road to Isabel's native village. We had to make frequent stops: two of the girls in our van kept being sick.

No one in Patricio's old van was sick, despite the fact that they were all either sitting on the floor or on crates. The van had nothing whatsoever in it. The noise and sheer discomfort inside this big rusty tin can down on its springs had to be experienced to be believed. But, then, what was noise and a little discomfort when you are being taken to a *merienda*, picnic, in the sierra? And how speedy the 25 m.p.h. when compared to being on the back of a mule.

Inside the *furgoneta* were also a number of five-litre *garrafas*. These we were going to fill from the various mountain springs near Isabel's village on our way to the picnic spot.

The spring waters gushing down the deep narrow ravines

roared and foamed and shone in the bright sunlight. It was already so hot that we were glad to stand in the cool shadow, welcoming the occasional burst of spray that fell upon us as we watched Isabel supervise the filling of the *garrafas*.

At each spring, Isabel carefully explained what the minerals in the water were good for: this for rheumatism, the village curse because of the humidity; this for arthritis, another curse; this for diabetes, which she herself suffered from; and so on.

I was irresistibly reminded of the herb stalls in Almería and other towns, with 30 to 40 sacks, all carefully labelled, and the ailments they would cure listed below their names – everything, apparently, except sudden death.

The picnic site was on the other side of a swiftly flowing rivulet. Patricio's battered van forded it triumphantly; mine (as I feared, due to past experience) conked out in the middle.

After a fraught pause, I saw the funny side, too, and joined in the general hilarity, ignoring the youngsters' pointed remarks about *las furgonetas inglesas*.

I got out, knee-deep in water, while Joan took the wheel. Patricio and the girls joined me at the back of the van, Patricio's face showing how much he agreed with the girls' opinion of our van. Despite the numbers of helpers, it was with some difficulty that we pushed the van out of the water, up the bank and on to the grass.

Patricio is one of the four village *pastores*, goatherds, so it was no surprise to me when, with a flourish, he produced a freshly-killed young *choto* for the *carne*. This was indeed a rare treat, as the general enthusiastic cries showed: prime young kids are expensive, only eaten, even by a goatherd's family, on very special occasions, such as this *merienda* with *lawingléh* as guests.

Patricio reminded me that the wine he served himself, me and Joan with came from Laujar, famous for its wines, and next to his wife's village. Nowhere, but nowhere in all the Alpujarras, did they produce better wines. Joan, as expected, refused.

The wine was certainly a pretty pink colour. I tasted it, wishing him *salud*, good health. It was thin, with that peculiar earthy dry undertow that many of these mountain wines have. I said I liked it, on the principle that anything was better than water, even Isabel's mineral-laden spring water.

The children had by now started the fire. Isabel placed the big trivet in position. She jointed the *choto* into the huge smoke-blackened frying pan. Poured jade-green virgin olive oil from her brother's *cortijo* in the hills above Laujar into it. Added a mixture of her own herbs. Grabbed the handful of spring onions and garlic her husband had tardily taken from his van. Sliced them, distributing the pieces.

Soon the delicious smell of cooking mingled with the mountain air, laden with scents carried to us on the gentle breeze from the surrounding scrub.

By now I was ravenous.

Isabelita and Mari Puri, helped (hindered?) by their cousins, had the bowls of salad ready, all the ingredients gathered that morning from their land — lettuce, cucumber, tomatoes, aubergines, artichoke, carrots, chickpeas cooked the day before in water from La Patrona, plus fat black olives, a gift from Isabel's brother. Patricio gave us each a *barilla*, short thick bar of bread, to begin with.

Never have we eaten a more delicious meal; truly a gourmet treat. Patricio kept filling my glass, assuring me that such a young wine had a low alcohol content – as if by then I cared. I knew Joan would drive home.

Relaxed and at peace, I reflected on the perverted and finicky ingenuity with which famous chefs seek to stimulate the jaded palates of their over-rich and underemployed clients, and contrasted such meals with this. But perhaps you have to be somewhat naïve even to make such a comparison, to think so highly of what was, after all (though prepared by a superb cook) an alfresco meal shared with open-hearted, unsophisticated friends? And shouldn't one always compare like with like!

It was only then that I began to worry about the van as we sat chatting in the sun. Would it have dried out enough to start? And if it had, how was I to get safely back through the water?

While I grimly pondered this, Isabel scoured the pan and the tin plates with sand from the river bottom and left them to dry in the sun.

Fortunately, I need not have worried. The bits and pieces had sufficiently dried out (I blessed the hot sun) for the van to start at once. And we could make a detour to avoid re-crossing the stream. 'Very necessary,' Patricio said, keeping a straight face, 'because these English vans are not as ... not used to these conditions as are ours.'

Two of the most important rituals in the village are the funeral, followed each year by the family's remembrance mass; and the *matanza*, the pig-killing.

It was our next-door neighbours who also gave us our first invitation to a *matanza*. We were pleased to accept.

Did this invitation set a precedent? Yes or no, we were from then on submerged under the number of invitations, all of which we felt duly obliged to accept. By the end of the *matanza* season, from the beginning of December to the end of February, we hoped we would never receive another invitation.

No one who invites you gives you any notice. The wife or one of her children comes to the door, tells you there's a *matanza* that day and we are to come. There could be no difficulty: we did not work in the fields, and so ...

The first intimation that Patricio was having a *matanza* was the screeches of his pig being urged out of the corral, a hideous sound that became all too familiar during the next three months.

The screeching had no sooner died away than Isabelita arrived with the invitation.

When were we to come? When we pleased. Now, if we wished, and Juanita could help the other women.

I decided to go at once; I was anxious to witness the whole event. Joan would come after the pig was killed.

Isabel, her daughters and three neighbours were busy about various tasks – taking the onions out of the sack, assembling the garlic, mixing the spices bought yesterday from the nearby town market, assembling the mincer. Each family, we learned later, had its own recipe, varying the spices and how they were mixed, the amount of onion and garlic, fat and salt, added to the minced

74

pork to make their own traditional brand of *morcilla*, black sausage, and *longaniza*, long pork sausage.

Isabel herself was keeping the fire going beneath a huge scoured-shiny pan filled with water (from La Patrona, of course) coming to the boil.

Patricio, his brother and three other men were holding the pig on the rough-stone patio, well away from the pan of boiling water, roped around each front foot and the upper jaw. Enrique, ex-butcher and now, in our neighbours' opinion, easily the best of the three village pig-stickers, stood, long knife in hand, ready to despatch the huge beast; which he did quickly and expertly.

A short wait for the bleeding to stop, some of the blood being caught to put in the black sausage; then '*Danos una mano*, Alberto, Give us a hand,' Patricio cried.

I stepped forward, helped to lift the huge carcass onto the well-scrubbed trestle-table, as much as the five of us could manage.

Enrique quickly and expertly gutted the pig. Now it was the turn of the women to empty and cleanse with lemon juice and water the intestines that would become the sausage skins. Joan arrived just in time to help peel the onions, to watch the garlic bulbs being gently roasted as if they were chestnuts before being peeled and sliced.

Before the men began to pour the boiling water over the carcass and to scrape the hair from the skin, Patricio said with satisfaction, '*Una gotita de vino*.' He lifted the leather bottle high above his head, let the wine pour in a stream from its narrow mouth into his own wide-open mouth, the wine disappearing down his throat without any discernible movement of his Adam's apple.

His companions followed suit, then passed the bottle to me, waited in smiling anticipation. I had not yet mastered the trick, knew I should spill more than I drank. And so I did. As I wiped the wine from my chin and chest, the onlookers, as is usual here, offered their varied advice on how to drink from the *bota*, an apt illustration of one of their favourite sayings: 'Here in Andalusia there's always one man working and four onlookers telling him how to.'

Enrique cut up the carcass. The legs and shoulder blades would be taken that day to be cured. The *jamones*, the cured hams, would then be hung with the sausages in an outhouse or a room where the air could freely circulate to provide the bulk of the meat to be eaten through the coming year.

The village hams are good, certainly, but not to be compared with the *jamón serrano*, the mountain ham, from such famous centres as Trevélez. One bar-restaurant there has the whole of its ceiling hung with hams, each with a little parasol attached to catch any drips. So close together are they, you cannot see a square inch of ceiling. You can choose the one you fancy. As the amiable proprietor unhooks it, his son stands by to replace it while yours is being sacked.

The most famous, most expensive hams, however, are to be found in Extremadura, the *Tierra abierta*, the Open Land, as the inhabitants fondly call it. There, in the cork-oak country, you come across the herds of small Iberian pigs, rooting for acorns with their long pointed snouts, their coats bright brown and grey-black, proof of their ancient lineage . . .

We last ate *jamón Iberico negro* in a bar in Jerez de los Caballeros, a truly lovely town near the Portuguese border. The owner of the bar was an enthusiast for this rare delicacy. On a gold chain around his neck he wore a huge acorn, mounted in gold. He took the chain off and handed it to me.

'This,' he said proudly, 'is the only food the pigs eat to produce the hams.' He thrust a skewer into one of the hams hanging behind the bar. 'Smell. *¡Qué aroma!*' We hastily agreed. He cut two tiny slices from the ham on the counter. 'Try it. There is nothing like it anywhere in the whole world!'

We chewed slowly and with relish. Solemnly agreed that he was right, making the necessary mental reservations. His pleasure was infectious; we felt privileged to be able to share it. Bought two (very pricey) sandwiches to eat later . . .

Isabel told Enrique how many cutlets and slices of pork to prepare, and how much to be put through the mincer for the sausages. A butcher would collect the rest later in the day; the quicker the better in this heat.

The chops and pork fillets would provide the deliciously

roasted basis for tomorrow's *matanza fiesta*. All the *familia* would turn up; in Patricio's case, 30 or more of them.

Were we to be invited? I need not have worried; of course we were.

The women took it in turns to put the pork through the mincer: though hard, this was women's work. The men sat on the patio in the sun, chatting, smoking, drinking, waiting for Isabel to serve (heaven knows how she found the time) the bowls of *puchero*, the thick meaty stew, the meat being Isabel's own rabbits.

We waited for the others to begin to eat. Following their example, we dipped our big spoons in the bowl in front of us. Fished about for the bits we fancied. Reached for the *barillas* of *pan tierno*, today's bread. Tore off chunks to dip in the stew. Used the same spoon to help ourselves to salad.

The *almuerzo*, midday meal, ended, we watched the pig, wide open, being suspended crosswise on the wooden framework kept for the job.

The women began to fill the sausage skins, squeezing the sausage meat out of nozzled bags before tying off the lengths to make each sausage.

Patricio used a pipe stem to blow up the pig's bladder. He tied it to a stick, handed it to one of the helper's little girls. Nostalgia, painfully sweet, flooded over me. How long ago was it, I asked myself, that I, too, had a pig's bladder blown up hard and attached to a stick to play with?

Although we had eaten in the partial shade of the vine, the sun blazed down from the usual flawless blue sky, and we found it quite hot enough, lightly dressed as we were. Our friends, however, were dressed in their winter gear – after all, it *was* winter, and what was the welcome heat from this sun compared to what they would get in summer? True, *lawingléh* found it hot, but they came from a land where in winter the snow lay in the very streets, or so they said.

By now we'd had enough. We said we must go. Thanked our hosts, to be met with the usual *de nada*, it's nothing.

Later Mari Puri brought a gift of liver and *morcilla*, blood sausage. She earnestly instructed us how to cook the liver and sausage, advice which Joan received in the spirit in which it was offered, keeping a very straight face. Other neighbours, we knew, would receive the same gift, to be returned when they had their own *matanza*.

Our next *matanza* was at the house of Juan José. Evedina, his daughter and Mari Puri's first cousin, slim, dark-eyed, dark-haired, 18 years old, sat next to us on the porch in the shade of an enormous tree. She pertly introduced herself. Proudly informed us her father was the richest man in the whole village – he possessed more fertile *parcelas* of land than anyone else. A father more modern also, compared to the other fathers (this said with a contempt she did not attempt to hide). He could easily afford the fees at Granada University. She was going to study to become a doctor, her heart's wish. Not a *practicante*, a medical assistant, like the one who comes on a Friday to the village to deal with the sick old people, but a fully qualified doctor.

'*Qué progreso*,' Joan said, glancing at me, well aware this was the expression I used to the villagers whenever they told me anything which seemed important to them as showing they were truly changing, even if only a little.

It was Evedina who, towards the end of the meal, seeing my plate empty once again, cried, '*Hombre*, have you no shame? Poor *Mamá*!'

Startled, I turned to Juan José. He explained that an empty plate at the end of a meal meant that the guest was still hungry, so the wife had at once, as was the custom here, to go and cook some more.

So much for my being taught in my childhood never to leave anything on the plate. I felt slightly ashamed at my lack of knowledge of this custom. Nevertheless, I thoroughly enjoyed the three extra slices of barbecued pork roasted on the ancient trivet Juan José's wife brought me. I ignored her daughter's disapproving glances.

*   *   *

78

A year after Evedina went to Granada University, neighbour Isabel came to see us. Hands tucked inside her pinny, she imparted her news. Evedina had transferred to Almería. She could not continue her doctor's course there. No, but – *ningun problema* – she had changed her mind. She was now going to become a teacher. Isabel caught Joan's enquiring look. 'Why did she change?' *Dios sabe*, only God knows, I do not. They say the course in Granada was too difficult. Yet she is, as Juan José has been saying since her birth, it seems, she is clever, *very* clever.'

When Isabel had gone, looking very pleased with herself with her parting shot that Juan José had told everyone his daughter was following in the educational footsteps of *lawingléh*, Joan said, 'At least her poor father and mother will not now have to make the journey to Granada every month carrying sacks of fresh vegetables and fruit.'

Another year passed. Neighbour Isabel asked us if we had been invited to the wedding. No. What wedding?

The wedding of the daughter of Juan José. Isabel smiled as she assured us that we would be. 'It is to their benefit to invite you. Otherwise, people will think you are not friends, and they would lose face.'

Evedina's wedding was the biggest the villagers could recall. The wedding feast, the most lavish: what must have been spent! I would willingly have testified to its lavishness.

Eduardo, the groom, was a short roly-poly young man with a carefully trimmed black beard, a newly-qualified doctor who lived in Almería. He was at present *sin trebajo*, without work, but had hopes that soon he would get a job. Evedina, for the first time in our brief acquaintance, looked both happy and satisfied. She even smiled at me.

Juan José, as thin as his wife was fat, unable to stand straight because of his arthritic spine and the long hours he still subjected it to in the fields – the words *hay que trabajar*, we must work, for ever on his lips – was plainly not at ease with us, but we had come, that was the important thing. He remembered too vividly, perhaps, his boast that his daughter was going to follow in the footsteps of our three daughters and acquire a profession. How clever she was. What talents she had. What a future she had ... He glanced at me. 'Like ... like your daughters,' he said, an intended compliment that fell flat, for how could he possibly have known? All the villagers, of course, *did* know what our daughters did – they had made it their business to ask early on in our acquaintance – but that was all.

I looked at Juan José, the richest man in the village, cheering on his guests, and felt sorry. The best laid schemes...

It was getting on for four years before Eduardo got a post in a hospital in Almería. During that time he and his wife lived in his father-in-law's house in the village. Eduardo grew smoother and glossier and plumper, while Evedina produced three *niños*, one boy and two girls. Why should Eduardo worry? Was not Juan José a man of considerable wealth who delightedly showered it on Evedina, himself and the *niños*?

Eduardo soon became the most popular young man by far in the village. Did he not promptly visit all who asked – no *mañana* with Eduardo, the villagers assured us, smiling at my well-known little joke, here tomorrow never comes – with his magic black bag which contained all that was necessary to look after you? And his prices? Certainly cheaper than those of the doctors in the town, so they were told by Juan José.

We understood their feelings. It was the first time they had been attended by a real doctor, unless in hospital. Otherwise, they did with the ministrations of the *practicante*, or Francisco the chemist, who was born and bred in the village and now had an important *farmacia* in the town.

The pig Enrique is to kill stands roped by jaw and feet before him. The long black screeches jetting out from its distorted throat are sacred music in his ears.

Enrique draws himself up to his full height. He is *endomingado*, dressed in his Sunday best, for this solemn ritual is his supreme moment of glory.

The neighbours gather round.

Enrique, dreaming of great Manolete, of brave Belmonte, approaches in his imagined suit of lights. The pig stands transfixed, not by the *torero*'s eye, but by the strong esparto ropes.

More neighbours arrive.

Enrique brandishes his long knife, his *estoque*, his killing sword: the neighbours draw in their breath as it catches fire in the sun.

To kill this *toro bravo* with a *recibiendo*, standing still to kill, or with a *volapie*, jumping in to kill? That is the question to be pondered and decided before he begins.

I must kill it today, Enrique silently tells himself, with supreme grace and skill, because here in my village there is a new rival. A conceited *muchacho*, a mere boy who boasts he is better than I. Only 30 years old he is – a crude Cordobés!

The villagers love to give, not only at *matanza* time, but throughout the whole year. We are often quite literally overwhelmed with the vegetables and fruit those who live in our *barrio* bring us. They cannot, it seems, give a small amount; a gift is not a gift unless it is huge.

So it is that when the folk in our *barrio* give us vegetables and fruit, it is always in what to us are enormous quantities. Big bags of tomatoes, aubergines, broad beans, French beans, oranges, lemons, courgettes, marrows, spring onions, and enough lettuce to feed an army of rabbits.

As for lemons and oranges, when Joan embarks on her marmalade-making, she needs absolutely fresh fruit. I go down to our neighbours who live at the bottom of Calle Cruces and who have a little orchard in front of their house. Short, fat, cheerful Bienvenida (a name which means 'welcome arrival') insists on helping me to pick the fruit. I emphasise I only want a *puñado*, a handful, of lemons this time. In vain: I go away with about as much as I can comfortably carry – and with some oranges thrown in for luck.

We discovered as time went on that the villagers have a number of reasons for giving.

Our immediate neighbours, and other neighbours such as Bienvenida, give for the sheer pleasure of giving and because they feel themselves friends. Others give because it does no harm to their prestige to be known to give to us.

Some of the older folk are convinced we are poor. If not, why are we not living in a chalet over the hill with the other foreigners? Why do I dress exactly like they do? Never once have they seen this *hombre* in a tie, let alone a suit. Moreover, as the ex-schoolmistress said with wonder in her voice, we treat everyone alike. Finally – most telling fact of all – we have no land.

There is one other reason, a religious one. When I regretfully told young Antonio I had nothing to give in return, he smiled indulgently. Said: '*Hombre*, you know what the *catecismo* says. *De nada*, I am but following what the *catecismo* tells me I ought to do – give.'

When Joan began making her marmalade, our neighbours questioned her closely. What was she doing? Why? Who ever heard of such a thing? Was there not much *mermelada de naranja*, so they'd heard, to be bought in the town by those who ate such things?

No one who has not tasted Joan's marmalade made from oranges and lemons picked the moment before can imagine the shock – yes, 'shock' is the word – of the sheer green-colour freshness on the unprepared palate. Little wonder, then, that she spent much time in the *casa* happily making it to take to our three daughters, and to some of our friends. Plenty of room in our faithful old Commer autosleeper for the jars as well as the sherries and wines.

Joan gave a simple pot to our neighbour Isabel for her and our other neighbours to try. She received it with no word of thanks. Joan's gift was never mentioned afterwards – the custom here, as I have mentioned before.

Shortly after Joan's most kindly-meant gesture. Yolandita, bright and attractive daughter of nearby neighbour Yolanda, came one morning with oranges, sugar and pan. Would Juanita teach her to *hacer la mermelada de naranja*?

When? Now, of course.

Joan warned me with a look to keep silent. Motioned me to go up to the studio and leave them in peace.

Did the lesson go well? Joan thought it had. Yolandita had gone away with a pan full of good marmalade, singing to herself, assuring Joan how much she and her *familia* would enjoy Juanita's marmalade.

Did Yolandita make any later? No. I'm sure because I cautiously asked her mother if she enjoyed her daughter's marmalade?

Mother Yolanda did not bother to hide her surprise. 'Not yet, Alberto, not yet. As you know, a fiancé has emerged. Now she is too busy to think of anything else. But she *will* make some, I'm sure.'

'*Mañana*,' I said, grinning.

They all know my views on this fatal word. She smiled, gladly shared the joke. '*Mañana, Alberto, mañana* for sure.'

I suggested we gave a pot to Isabel, Miguel Cuba's wife and Alfredo's aunt. We visited regularly. Miguel was something of a philosopher and had a fund of good stories, which we much enjoyed.

Joan gave the pot to Isabel. Explained what it was and its provenance.

Isabel peered suspiciously at it. Ordered Miguel to get a spoon. Removed the cover. Held the pot away from her as if it were going to bite her. Brought it close enough to gaze into it. Scraped out a very little on the spoon. Pointed. '*Cáscaras*,' she said in a tone of infinite scorn.

Yes, Joan explained, they were skins, but they were part of a good traditional *mermelada de naranja*.

Isabel shook her head. Not for her. She tipped back what she had just taken out. Replaced the cover. Handed back the pot to Joan. '*No nos gusta*,' she said, including poor Miguel in her statement of dislike.

We cut our visit short. My mistake, my mistake, I earnestly assured Joan once we were out in the street.

I need not have worried. She smiled, shrugged, said, 'Not to worry. All part of life's rich pattern – to coin a phrase.'

9

When Joan bought our house, *invernaderos*, the familiar plastic greenhouses (the word itself means 'winter quarters') had not come into use in our valley. No plastic lining the minor road to our village; no plastic in our *vega* or perched on the surrounding hill slopes.

Then the villagers toiled away growing huge quantities of tomatoes and lettuce, the two staple crops, to find only too often the price they could get was so low – as little as five *pesetas* a kilo for tomatoes – that the crop was not worth the carting. Seeing the huge mounds of tomatoes and lettuce dumped in the dry river bed to rot in the hot sun pained us, made us rail against *los intermediarios*, the middlemen, as the villagers did.

The villagers were reluctantly forced to adopt the only course open to them: go into hock with the bank, even though they would be paying 13 to 15 per cent interest, and hire one of the specialised gangs that toured the region to make them *invernaderos*. An adequate-size one would cost 12–15,000 pounds sterling; little wonder, that when you asked them how they were getting on, their invariable reply was: '*Trabajamos por el banco.*' Yet, working for the bank or not, they prospered; and we were as pleased for them as if they were relatives.

There was a price to be paid, however. You can imagine what it is like working beneath plastic in the fiery summer sun: the stifling heat, and what air there is often filled with one of the sprays needed to produce perfect produce that would pass to be exported, and so earn a satisfactory return. It was the village women, and especially the adolescent girls, who paid the price the plastic houses exacted; their hitherto unblemished complexions were ruined, although in time things improved.

Soon large tracts of the valley were covered by plastic greenhouses. The *agricultores* were now producing larger crops. Mules and donkeys were no longer adequate for carrying the crops to one of the packing stations five kilometres or so away, and they were compelled to buy *furgonetas*, the word a diminutive of *furgón*, a van, another instance of the Andaluz's passion for using a diminutive where one exists, and of inventing one if it does not exist in Castilian.

Everyone kept their mules, their principal use now to plough the land. As Juan White Mule was fond of telling me: '*Hombre, máquinas*, machines. What use are *máquinas* here in our *vega*? They destroy the structure of the soil.' Here he winked. 'And they drink money. No, Alberto, mules for me. Light on the soil, dunging it as they go, and pulling the best ploughshare ever invented.'

And when I remember that the *vega* has been under constant cultivation since Phoenician times, 3,000 years ago (our village was then a port), I have to admit Juan knows what he is talking about.

When visitors moan, as they so frequently do, about the plastic, Joan tartly reminds them that the locals have to earn their living, and that it is *their* land and they can do as they like with it. People who can't stand the plastic have the remedy in their own hands – not that we welcomed the change, we hastily admit to each other.

We were determined, as I've said, to keep our *casa* as much as possible as it was originally. So it was that in those early days, and for a number of years thereafter, we limed the walls inside as well as out, as was the custom.

We had a problem, though. The back walls of living room and chief bedroom are of solid rock, and whitewash does not stay on it for a decent length of time. Often in the morning, the *azulejos* on the living-room floor would be covered with what appeared as fine snow from distant Sierra Gador that had miraculously found its way in.

The part of the wall in front of which we sat for breakfast

showed the solid rock, despite our frequent limings, although we soon gave this up.

All who passed could see the mosaic behind our head; all expressed their concern; all had a solution.

'Paper the walls. How pretty wallpapers are these days. Such patterns, such bright colours. They of the *chaletes* over the hill use them. Go and see.'

'Build a brick wall, a *camera de aire*. The air between it and the back wall will keep away the humidity, the cause of all the trouble. Another advantage, it will make the room neater and better to look at. That old rough plastered wall was good enough for those who lived here before you, but . . .'

Making a *camera de aire* was Juan White Mule's persistent suggestion. And he knew a mason, a relative, who would do the job cheaply for me.

'Paint the walls with this new plastic paint. The *humedad*, humidity, in the town in the houses by the sea is worse than it is here. My cousin has had her walls done, and that cured the problem.'

It was this last, and by far simplest, suggestion that we eventually adopted, but we were so besotted with our *casa* that we were for some years content to go on as we were.

In our bedroom, the tiny avalanches were more frequent than in the living room, and the lime lay like lace along the edge of our carpet's lustrous blue.

The back wall itself was to us a work of art, at least the equal of many of those abstracts the galleries were showing.

Occasionally, conscience smote us. Oughtn't we do something about walls which were, after all, walls from which the lime kept falling? Not works of art, but just an eyesore, if not a disgrace.

Before we put out the light, we'd agree that soon we really *would* do something about it. *Mañana*. Much comforted, need I say, by the knowledge that here in Andalusia tomorrow never comes.

The path across from our front door ends in a wall. Below the wall is a stand of prickly pears, and below that the ground slopes steeply down to the *vega*.

We love to see the fruits appear all along the edges of the great oval prickly leaves. Grow. Change from green to scarlet to scarlet-yellow as they ripen. The villagers no longer eat them. Too much trouble: the fruits are covered in hair-like prickles which, once they get into your fingers, are the very devil to get out. We pick and peel them in gloves. They are worth our trouble, being deliciously sweet and juicy.

Sometimes our neighbour, Patricio Pastor, lets his goats pass through the prickly pears. Their leathery mouths protect them from the prickles, and with their tough teeth they take oval bites from the edges of the leaves, leaving the white inner flesh exposed.

We accept this spoilage. Are grateful that Patricio, out of consideration for our incomprehensible idea that the *chumberas* on our bit of land by the side of the house are worth looking at (beautiful, even!), does not massacre them with his machete as he regularly does on the hillside to supplement his herd's sparse diet. Grateful also that he prevents his goats from eating the plants in our little 'garden' – when he remembers, that is.

The village is alive with cats. Not domesticated, as are our cats. These cats are born outdoors, and live and die outdoors. They maintain their distance. Keep a sharp eye on you as you pass. Know they are always a possible target for a kick or a stone.

Yet if we are out of the house for a few moments, leaving the door open, we often find a cat ensconced in one of the easy chairs. Always a she; and out she darts at sight of us. When, if at all, I wonder, and then how many generations ago, did one of her female ancestors live in a house?

The cats exist on what they can catch, and on what the women throw out, principally fish-guts and the remains of meals. Most families here eat fish three or four times a week; some, seven days a week. The fishman brings only small fish – in season, anchovies, sardines, squid, octopus, mussels, red mullet, mackerel – at a price the villagers will pay: big fish are far too dear!

We are always astonished at what splendid specimens these

cats are and what superb condition they are in. Our prickly pears are home, fortunately, to a beautiful ginger tabby. Of her present two kittens, the female is a small replica of herself, the male a bright black-and-white. Their behaviour we find a perpetual delight.

They wait below the wall in the morning for Joan to throw out her scraps. They have to be quick; the sound of the plate scraping brings other cats at the run. At night, after a lean day, they wait outside our door while dinner is cooking. They have foraged along Calle Cruces and elsewhere all day. Surely now such good smells must result in something for them if they wait long enough?

The mother is an excellent mother. Lies below the wall in the sun and allows the kittens to climb all over her, paw her, play with her tail. Only rarely does she lose patience with them, spit at them, sends them scurrying off. When she wants to nap undisturbed, she climbs a prickly pear and lies on one of its leaves, oblivious of the prickles. The other advantage of being there is that she is safe from passing dogs – all dogs are encouraged from their earliest years to harass cats whenever they can.

Our beautiful ginger tabby gives her kittens first go at our scraps and brings the occasional mouse for them to play with and practise their hunting skills.

Surely, we suppose, feeding them as we do, they will become friendly, allow us to come near enough to stroke them? But no, they maintain only a wary truce.

The mating season begins in February. Formidable toms arrive as our tabby is coming into heat. Sinisterly patient and apparently casual, they bide their time. No use, they know, approaching this ginger lady until she decides she is ready.

During the day, their blood-curdling opera is often quenched by well-directed buckets of water. The most impassioned and sustained arias, however, are reserved for the night. One of their favourite stages, alas, is the hillside behind our bedroom.

Mission innumerable times accomplished, our tabby comes back to her home worn out, bedraggled, but with the triumphant air of a job well done.

Soon the black-and-white male kitten leaves to *buscar la vida*,

Partial view of the village from our terrace

Our house, Calle Cruces (page 26)

View of the village from the terrace with Maria Passion-Pants outside her door (page 69)

On our terrace with daughter Janet and granddaughter Claire

Agave in front of our house, with below two potato patches in the *vega* (page 91)

Great-grandmother, aged 93, with great-grandson, aged one (page 131)

Patricio's goats leaving the corral (page 100)

An abandoned house (page 174)

seek a new life, the expression the more squeamish villagers use when they take an unwanted dog into the hills to abandon it, rather than turning it out, kicking it away from the door, or shooting it.

The female kitten, we are pleased to observe, stays with her mother, acts now the part of the loving companion. She will stay, too, we find, to help bring up the two new kittens, one a pretty grey tabby, the other a plain black, redeemed from ugliness by the white tip to its tail.

We are certain we know the sire of the black kitten. He is a tattered-eared, square-headed male with a tail like a well-used pipe-cleaner. Too old, you might think, to be pursuing his lifelong purpose; but obviously he has still something to spare.

We know when one of the bitches in our *barrio* is coming into season by the arrival of their most ubiquitous suitor.

His home is in a *cortijo* in the sierras about ten kilometres from us; it was there that we first saw him. He did not bark frenziedly at us as we passed, as such dogs usually do, having made up his mind when he sighted us that we were harmless.

He is a short-coated brown mongrel with a wall-eye; this causes him to carry his head sideways as if he were listening to disembodied voices whispering in his right ear. A smallish dog, about nine inches from pad to shoulder, he is yet most magnificently hung, a classic case of little jockey, big whip.

How he manages to be first into the mating ring from his distant *cortijo*, I cannot imagine; but first he always is. Nothing to do with scent, surely? A sixth sense seems the only possible explanation.

No one keeps their bitch indoors when she comes on heat: whatever for? So when she is coming into season, she wanders everywhere, attended closely by anything up to ten males of all shapes and sizes, our wall-eyed friend being *primus inter pares*.

Wall-eye has struck up a friendship with a village dog almost as ubiquitous. Like has doubtless called to like, and there is a friendly rivalry to be first, so to say, at the fountain.

This dog is a magnificent Alsatian. Noble head, muscled body, thick coat and tail, all would earn high marks in the show ring. But the legs – the legs are only half the length they should be. The effect is so comic you have to look twice to make sure you're not seeing things. From what dam did he spring? I often wonder. And what animal equivalent of the ambitious milkman must have crossed her path?

The children find the prolonged public matings highly amusing, especially when their favourite little dog, glossy-coated and chestnut-coloured, attempts to mate with some long-legged female.

On one memorable occasion, Wall-eye mated with a young bitch. Eventually, he swung off her, but they remained joined, the children howling with delight or derision, we could not tell which. Alerted by the din, one of the mothers appeared, struck Wall-eye a solid blow with her broom, but it was the poor bitch that screamed as they abruptly parted company.

A little bitch we know has her home among the prickly pears opposite Bienvenida's orchard, which is where I go to beg for Joan's marmalade lemons and oranges.

The bitch, with a Jersey-cow-coloured coat, white collar, paws and tip of tail, was born among the prickly pears and has never been in a house. When three of her mother's litter of four were taken by people who wanted a puppy, she was left, being the smallest and weakest.

Soon after, the mother disappeared. Soft-hearted Bienvenida saw to it she had enough food. The little puppy flourished. Older, she did not depend entirely on Bienvenida, but became an expert hunter and scavenger.

She has reared five fine litters, and has such a sweet nature that she has been accepted by the families in that part of our *barrio* as belonging there. Confident of her place in everyone's affections, she even allowed us to pet her, lying on her back and putting up her paws as if she were someone's pampered pet.

We now bring her bones, we admire her so much, full of wonder that a dog who has never been in a house could act in this way.

That she and the cats can live so well outdoors is, incidentally, a tribute to our climate.

Between our prickly pears and the wall are two agave plants. Last year there were only the basal clumps of bluish-green sword-blade leaves, six feet or more in height, and six inches thick. They are edged with such strong spines, with an especially cruel one at the tip, that even the goats cannot tackle them. The goat-herds are forced to chop them in pieces and hack off the spines before feeding them to their herds.

This year the agaves have sent up fleshy, fibrous flower stalks, more trunks than stalks, 20 feet high and 18 inches in diameter. The short side stalks which jut out from the top third of the main stem bear clusters of buds which break into scented greeny-yellow blossom.

The agave is also known as the American aloe or century plant. The latter name was bestowed on it because it was thought to flower only once a century, instead of every ten to twenty years.

On the hillside at the back of our house there are seven agave clumps. When, we ask ourselves, wishing it to be so, will they send their great stems suddenly steepling skywards? (One soon did.)

The two agaves in front of the house are already leaning perilously towards the slope below them. They are shallow rooted, susceptible to the wind. Soon, we know, they will topple.

We shall miss them. So will the birds, now using them as a favoured perch and soon to feast after the flowers have seeded.

10

A flock of sparrows roost under the eaves of Patricio's corral. Not nearly as tame as our English sparrows, but even noisier. Handsomer, though, with their bold black bibs.

The camp we stayed on when our caravan had a puncture was shaded by fine eucalyptus. At twilight, these would resound with the noisy excited chattering of birds. But what birds?

'*Gorriones*,' the proprietor said, yet I found it hard to believe that they really *were* sparrows, such were their numbers and the din they were making.

Our sparrows have a rival when they dash down to devour our crumbs. This is the long-tailed grey wagtail, a handsome bird, yellow-breasted and grey-backed, its tail constantly in motion as befits its name. Their habitat is near water. What the two pairs that haunt Calle Cruces think they are doing here in this dusty area, I do not know. They are not at all shy and obviously quite at home.

Some time ago a pair of little egrets made their home farther up the river valley which divides the *vega*. They thrived. The years passed, their numbers increased, and now there is a colony of upwards of 20.

They regard our *vega* as their own. Regularly glide gracefully down to graze. At least, that is what they appear from our *terraza* to be doing, but they are in reality spearing insects as the heron spears fish. Daisy-white, white-crested, yellow-footed, their heron-like movements as they concentrate on the job in hand is fascinating.

I feared at first they would be shot. But no, they are allowed to stalk about in peace. Occasionally they perch to rest in the fruit trees that fringe the plots – exotic fruit indeed – each pair as their numbers increase keeping close to each other.

When I asked a neighbour why no one shot them, he stared at me in astonishment, but I found his reply most welcome despite its tone.

'*Hombre!* Are you mad? Shoot them? Waste a cartridge on birds that are all wings and feet? Nothing at all to eat on the carcass. Never!'

Fortunate birds! One hard winter, a flock of lapwings, unknown in our valley, were driven south and made their way here to rest awhile and find something to eat, perhaps.

Instant response: three neighbours came out with their shotguns. Three shots, three dead lapwings. There was a scramble down to the *vega* to bring them back. Examine them. Finger their slender black crests, their lime-white breasts. Stretch their rounded-fingered wings, awakening the iridescent gleam that lay hidden among the black.

'*Que bonito!*' cried the grouped children. 'How pretty!'

No more flesh on them, of course, than on the egrets: their strangeness was their undoing.

The colours of the birds leading their busy lives are doubly welcome in this sun-punished landscape; our *terraza* is the perfect viewing balcony, field glasses our second pair of eyes.

The bright streaked-yellow serins are ground feeders that stay till you almost tread on them as you walk, before they protest sibilantly as they flutter away. The equally bright siskins love to perch near the house, displaying their greeny-yellow markings, as do the yellowhammers themselves.

Black wheatears flash by, their white rump shining. Starlings, too, that have cast off their eyed chainmail and appear in drab reach-me-downs, but just as swaggering and noisy as their British counterparts.

Wren-tiny birds we have not identified home in, as autumn comes, on the pomegranate tree that grows below the wall directly in front of our house. They and the coloured butterflies (yes, butterflies also) bury themselves in the split fruit, gorge on the sweet juice and flesh.

In winter the twiggy tree, more large bush than tree, looks to be on its last legs. We anxiously watch in spring for the bronzed young leaves to appear, followed by the dainty inconspicuous flowers. They will set seed, we know, to produce a lavish crop of fruit.

Joan is passionately fond of pomegranates. She picks and devours them steadily as they ripen, leaving a few (very few) for the birds and butterflies.

The tree belongs to Patricio, our next-door neighbour. He has given us sole right to its crop: 'Who, *cielos*, heavens, wants to eat those great fat scarlet *granada* and be choked with pips?'

When the swallows arrive at the beginning of February ready to build their nests in the corrals or up in the topmost rooms where often the sausages and hams are hung to dry in the air that flows through the open windows, they sit in pairs on the washing lines next door and make their sweet, soft, companionable music, a perpetual delight to us.

A delight, too, to watch them hunting. They sweep up and down Calle Cruces, often low enough to make you duck. Over our heads also as we sit on the *terraza*, and close enough to our eyes to make us blink.

The noisy sparrows, from their balcony of pomegranate and almond trees, do not heed them. But we feel privileged from our own balcony to gaze at their blue-glinting beauty as they perform their incredible feats on the ice rink of the air. Entranced, we sit without moving, without talking, at peace momentarily with the world.

Before the matchless swallows arrive, the stubby sand martins and the drawn-bow swifts come, the air alive with their thread-like cries.

We never see the high-flying swifts without recalling one day at twilight in the *judería*, the Jews' quarter, in Córdoba. One moment, the sky was a flawless dusky blue; the next, miraculously covered by a false night of keening swifts: a breathtaking and unforgettable sight.

There is only one other bird sound more softly musical, more loving, than that of the paired swallows who chat as they momentarily rest from their insect swoops on the lines of our neighbours' houses. We heard this once and once only in mid–Spain. We had motored over one of Wellington's bridges and pulled off down into a grassy hollow to have lunch. We settled outside the van and began to eat. Then from the sandy bank a few yards to our left we heard these subdued, musical, flute-like sounds. The birds, a cloisonné of daffodil and chestnut above, of cerulean and fawn below, were making brief circular sorties from the bank, while their companions on the bank kept up their soft murmurings.

We sat for a long time entranced. How beautiful were these bee-eaters. And never had we chanced across such an amiable company.

Each year we wait for our solitary kestrel to take up his winter abode in the red-brick bell tower of the church, *La Iglesia de Nuestra Virgen de las Angustias*.

From there each day, we watch this magnificent blue-headed male as it rapidly quarters the *vega* and the surrounding hills, suspends its clean flight, hovers 20 feet above the earth, wings whirring, black-barred blue tail fanned wide, before it sights its prey then swoops, talons spread, upon small mammal or insect.

Another winter visitor is the great grey shrike, blunt-headed, cruel-beaked, back black-and-white-patterned. The size of a blackbird, but bulkier. Also a formidable predator, it often perches on a tree on top of the hill behind our house and gazes sinisterly down before swooping on some luckless little bird or mammal.

Extremadura, the province which glories in its *jamón serrano negro*, is also the land of predators.

There, motoring through the limitless plains, the barren hills, we have seen the sky above our heads alive with predators – hawks big and small, red kites, buzzards, griffon vultures, and prominent among them the kingly golden eagle – each etching its own immemorial patterns against the bright blue.

These distant-horizoned plains, these sparsely clad hills, apparently empty of life, what a dense population of small creatures they must in fact support to feed such flocks of predators.

Apropos of our difficulty in identifying some birds, trees and flowers, the villagers have no interest in naming them. And those names they do know, as with the fish we all buy, are mostly dialect words, not to be found in any dictionary other than Maria Moliner's massive two-volume *Diccionario de Uso del Español*, published by Gredos. So we have to rely on the standard bird, tree and flower reference books, which we sometimes find lacking, as we do the Moliner when the word is a local neologism.

The housewives, not interested in birds except canaries, are very fond of flowers. They fill the ledges behind their *rejas*, window bars, with plants of all kinds, as well as the borders of their patios. No fancy ceramic coloured flowerpots here, as you see everywhere in tourist areas; any old tin of any colour, size and shape is pressed into service alongside the occasional ordinary brown flowerpot. All the stranger, then, they have no interest in the names of the plants and flowers they grow in such profusion.

They do not even name their animals. Mules are Mulo or *Mula*, donkeys *Burro* or *Burra*. Even their dogs rarely get named. As for cats, they live outdoors, so belong to nobody in particular. Useful scavengers and to keep the vermin down, but that is all . . . The only cat they know with a name belongs to old Gador. It lives in the house with her. Can you wonder some of the children think she is a witch?

Of course, my favourite dog had a name – Ofelia. Yet when Rosa Sol acquired another dog to replace Ofelia, I had to urge her to name the tiny fawn, furry puppy. Eventually, she did: Benito. Appropriate enough, I thought, studying the pug-nosed, prognathous little creature. When I mentioned Mussolini to her, it did not ring a bell. The name, she said, she had plucked out of the clouds.

Many families own canaries, hung in minute cages on the façade of their house during daylight hours, where the birds rival each other in the frequency, loudness and length of their bursts of song.

Is it the long hours of sunlight that encourages them to sing so often, their full-throated singing to be so mellifluous?

The old men sit in the shade, listen entranced by what awakened bitter-sweet nostalgic memories?

*   *   *

Spring is the season when the gypsies become busy trapping birds.

One of the areas they frequent is a piece of wasteland in the *vega* directly in front of our house. The only reason this has lain fallow for so long, so my neighbours tell me, is that it is *tierra muerta*, dead earth. And why should it be so when it is surrounded by such fertile land? No one seems to know. What they do know is that nothing will grow on it. It is not worth buying or renting, of no interest to them or anybody else.

The *gitanos*, usually a gross father and two adolescent sons, arrive with their cages of decoy birds and their limed sticks. They carefully choose the sites to erect the slender deadly traps, sit silently, basking contentedly in the sun, awaiting the coming of the poor innocent victims.

It is the lean sons who dash whooping forward when a bird gets stuck. Gently pluck off the bird. Deposit it in the empty cage by their father's side.

The father and his family live in Calle Principal; their next-door neighbours are also *gitanos*. The outside walls of their houses are spattered with minute cages. A few contain canaries; most, a gamut of goldfinches, chaffinches, greenfinches, linnets, yellowhammers, siskins, and even a robin or two they have at various times trapped.

Cruelty? They have no concept of what we mean by the word. (Nor, I may add, do the majority of the other villagers.)

On the gypsies' flat roof – all the houses have flat roofs where the washing is hung – they have built a bird room. By the end of the trapping season, it usually contains upwards of two dozen birds.

At least, I comfort myself, the enforced captives have room to fly about a bit.

And what do they do with all these birds? Those they do not select for themselves for their song, or cannot sell, they in due course eat.

We sit quite still, our picnic finished, and watch the fieldmouse coming towards us.

We are too enormous for the gleaming blackness of your beads of eyes to take in. Unaware, you trickle right up to us, searching for food.

I lift my foot and you drift under it, safe in the roofed cool dark. You creep out and Joan places a piece of bread close to your etched front paws. At once you hug it and, hunched up, begin to chew at starving speed, fur grey and fine as ashes, shoulders bright as acorn.

You devour the bread and, thistledown in a gentle breeze, you roll lightly, slowly, to the forest of the hedge.

We're glad you're equally unaware of the hawk that by day hunts you, of the phantom owl by night, and live in such serene innocence between a death and a death.

The air suddenly darkens, although far too early for twilight. Is it the tilt of the sky's mirror towards the quenched sun, or is it my own keen apprehension as the taloned death above me quarters the scrubland?

The hawk dives, is lost for a second in the bushes, then stretches into the averted air, the ripped fieldmouse held dying, while its warm blood begins to stain its own suspended hands.

11

It is a treasured daily ritual, this fetching water from the fountain. How often have we heard the villagers say how fortunate they are that La Patrona is situated *above* all the houses. And well above the cemetery, *gracias a Dios*. Were this not so, who knows what would have happened to our pure water? We had only to remember the plague that took nearly all the people in that settlement up the valley to imagine what might have happened to us.

Girls are at the fountain with their pitchers. Firm-fleshed, cheeks glowing, they chatter incessantly as they wait their turn. They see the old woman coming and their chattering dies away.

Gador comes painfully slowly up the steep, winding path, one hand resting on her arthritic hip. She is in full mourning garb, the *luto* widows wear permanently from the day their husband dies. The dark skin is stretched tightly over her face, the colour of the chipped pitcher she grasps in her gnarled hand. Moro, her black cat, walks at her side, tail erect.

The girls move away, jerking their heads in her direction. One whispers, 'Witch, witch, get away from here.' Another makes the sign of the cross and whispers, 'The cat, look, I'm frightened.'

The sun is fiery; the indifferent fountain murmurs. The old woman reaches it, stops to hear what it is saying. Yes, she hears her husband's name, repeats it aloud: 'Vitor . . . Vitor . . .' The girls huddle together, ask themselves what she is saying. One suggests she is cursing them; and another agrees.

Gador is still, eyes shut against the blinding light, and offers her usual prayer: 'Thank you, *Señor*, for Moro, my only company.'

Above her, the leaves of the aspen lift in the suddenly awakened breeze and grow pale. Near her, the fruits of the prickly pear are bright as blood being freshly shed.

The girls go and shelter from the sun in the tawny shade of the tall tamarisks. One crosses herself, and they begin to whisper again.

Gador, pitcher on hip, makes her insecure way homewards, her mind filled with thoughts of her husband, the perpetual question – 'Why, Vitor, did you leave me?' – still unanswered.

By her front door, next to the geraniums bright as a blessing, Moro stands and purrs his welcome.

When the full moon comes out, the village girls sigh, lost in dreams of the mistress moon.

When the full moon comes out, the children stare fixedly at the snowy face of the old man who still lives in the moon.

When the full moon comes out, the old men hug themselves, praying, their bed cold, to the goddess moon.

When the full moon comes out, the widows refuse to look at the reminder of lost youth and lost happiness.

When the full moon comes out, we sit on the *terraza*, gaze enchanted at her golden beauty, her cohort of brilliant stars.

There are four herds of goats in our village, ranging from 50 to 150 strong. Patricio's, let out from the nearby corral, seem compelled to drop their shiny black currants in front of our house as they pass. As soon as they are gone, Joan comes out and sweeps them away; she doesn't want them brought indoors on the bottom of someone's boots.

José, the oldest goatherd, is well over 80, as far as he can tell. He still wears the remnants of the old green velvet suit, once his Sunday best and now the colour of the scrub itself. On his sockless feet are the sandals made from an old motor tyre. I look down and wonder at the toughness of feet that can walk up mountainsides for miles and miles in such harsh, unsympathetic things.

He never carries a whip, as some goatherds do; in particular one young bearded man who comes into our valley and seizes every chance to lash any goat that strays. José carries only a sling, which he can still use expertly; a stone from it will land near the wilful goat and bring her promptly back to the herd.

We find him one hot day sitting on the scrub of a nearby hillside. I seize my chance to chat, knowing what the subject would be. We exchange courteous greetings. He offers me a hand-rolled cigarette, which I politely refuse: '*No fumo, José, como sabes bien.*'

He lights up, draws the smoke deep down, sighs it out in complete satisfaction. Not for him the amazingly cheap fags the villagers smoke in such quantities, but even cheaper ones of his own, herbs mixed in with the tobacco.

He glances at me fondly, and I know he is ready to chat.

'Look at my great buck goat, Alberto, see his long black beard. He's able to cover all the goats in my herd, all 50 or more. Before him, I had two billies, but now I need only him, and –'

Here he pauses dramatically, glances fleetingly at Joan, although he seemingly ignores her during our conversation, enjoying as I am the knowledge that I know what is coming next, a little game we play.

'And my billy, he nearly always fathers twins, triplets sometimes. You can imagine how envious are the other *pastores*, they who laughed at me when I went up into the mountains to buy him. Laughed, too, at the price I paid. But now . . .'

There is no need for me to say anything; he knows he has my full attention.

He gestures to where his dogs lie, tongues out, in the shade of a boulder.

'You know my two dogs, mother and son. Good dogs, they know their business, obey me at once. I feed them well, not like some *pastores* . . . And this *sequía*, every year now we get this drought, not like in the old days when plenty of *agua* fell –'

I smile at his use of the word *agua*, water; they have no other word for rain.

'This *sequía* . . . Pasture becomes scarcer. I have to go farther now to find it. And at times I have to buy grain, for how else can I keep the milk flowing? And for me, the hillsides become steeper, the stones sharper and more treacherous, than once they were . . .'

'We are all growing older,' I say; cold comfort, I know, but I can think of nothing else to say.

'*Si, Alberto, tengo muchos años*, I have many years. More than 80, of that I am certain.'

He is silent for so long that I conclude he has finished. When he begins to speak again, there is a note of resignation in his voice I have not heard before.

'Every now and again, Alberto, I sit and chat with *El Señor* up there *en los cielos*. Without *El Señor*, yes, I should be on my own, my sons have left the village, and *mi mujer* is dead . . .'

I pat his arm in sympathy. Poor old chap . . . But his next remark reassures me that all is as before.

'But, Alberto, look at my great *macho cabrio con la barba negra. ¡Qué hombre!*'

I do not need even to glance at him to know he is smiling.

There on the spine of the hill above us goats incise shapes as familiar to our psyche as fabled unicorns.

That great buck's outline palaeolithic man drew by torchlight on the dark walls of his sacrificial caves. Necessary magic to ensure unabated fertility, renewal of life.

You would think as you watch the slow, careful mules making their way along the paths into the *vega* that they could not possibly gallop. Trot, yes, for you would occasionally have seen an impatient youngster kicking his into a trot for at least a short distance. But you would be wrong, because you have not seen Miguel's notorious mule.

Once a week he is tethered in the *vega* on the stretch of *tierra muerta*, dead land, nobody seems to own. His tether is long, and he uses it to find what scanty pasture he may. This *tierra muerta* lies between one of the *acequias* laid down by the Moors all those centuries ago and now a concreted channel, and the high grey wall of the cemetery, with above it the brick tower, a soft beige colour crowned with crooked tiles, of *La Iglesia de Nuestra Virgen de Las Augustias*.

Soon the mule, as we anticipate, will provide us with his usual entertaining spectacle. After he has grazed a while, he rolls in the dust of one of the many bare patches, kicks his feet vigorously as if to loosen his joints, rises, just as vigorously shakes himself and walks slowly to the end of the tether. There he gazes around him, then rears and tugs, rears and tugs until he has wrenched the tether loose. This he always manages, no matter how long the pin on the other end of the tether.

He lifts his head, and a triumphant sound issues from his powerful throat. He kicks his heels in the air and begins to gallop, yes, really *gallop*. Fortunately, there's a narrow path around this part of the *vega*. He keeps to this, his racetrack, thus avoiding the crops in the plots that edge it.

Around and around he goes at what to us is an incredible speed, only stopping when he is thoroughly out of breath.

Suddenly, Miguel comes round the corner of the cemetery wall, in his hand a long cane. The mule gazes at it; he thinks, perhaps (the triumph of hope over bitter experience), that it's a piece of sugarcane for him, his favourite titbit.

As Miguel draws nearer, the mule snorts and begins to gallop again. He will, as we know, stop, wait until Miguel is within reach, then gallop off again. This will go on until he misjudges his wait, and Miguel, by now mad as fire, can seize the tether.

As Miguel begins to wield the *caña*, the mule opens his jaws, gives voice to a cry, harsh, shrill, long-suffering, a cry that fills the village and echoes among the surrounding hills before it vanishes in a long and trembling sigh.

12

L.P. Hartley begins the prologue to *The Go-Between* with this memorable sentence: 'The past is a foreign country: they do things differently there'.

This is so true of Andalusia – a foreign country with a foreign culture more of the East than the West.

Although thousands upon thousands of people of other races live along the coast, clustering in towns like Málaga, you have only to think of the processions that take place in Holy Week with their spontaneous *saetas* sung by onlookers as the Virgin Mary passes; of the religious hysteria and the flagellations; of the spectacle (not sport) of the *corrida de toros*; of the plays and poems of Federico García Lorca, to realise how true this is.

I think of the processions in our village. However lash-up, these are endowed with the same arcane qualities as the grand processions in the great cities of Spain.

We always witness the *Noche Buena*, Christmas Eve, procession. Scheduled to begin at 7 p.m., it is nearly an hour late, as usual.

The small group of men outside *La Iglesia de Nuestra Virgin de las Angustias* during the service will join their families when they emerge.

We wait at the upper end of Calle Principal, the few remaining paving stones on its surface long since shattered, a good vantage point before the procession turns to wind its way up through the village.

Ah, here it comes.

Heading the procession, doña Antonia and doña Pasión, the

two old ladies who look after the church. Antonia is dressed in a long frilled white dress, Pasión all in black. Their tall elaborate mantillas seem precariously balanced. We can barely make out their faces beneath their veils. The lit candles in their hands are of formidable size.

Behind them is the dark-skinned, scourged, bloodstained Christ, his tearful face contorted beneath his crown of thorns, his robe by contrast imperial purple and richly hemmed.

He is borne aloft on the shoulders of young village men, honoured to be chosen for this taxing task.

Lorca's poem, *Saeta*, goes through my mind:

> Dark Christ
> changed
> from Judean lily
> to Spanish carnation.
>
> *Look where he comes!*
>
> From Spain.
> Sky clear and dark,
> sun-tortured earth,
> and streams where water
> flows sluggishly.
> Dark Christ,
> with your lank angry hair,
> your jutting cheekbones
> and your blank eyes.
>
> *Look where he goes!*

The village women, old and young, children on foot and in arms, follow. They carry slim lighted candles. The men, mostly agnostic or non-believers, look slightly uncomfortable.

The women and children chatter, smile at the spectators: is not tomorrow the birthday of *El Señor Jesús*?

The older women peer at those who line the path. They note who are present, who absent. At least those present are showing some respect. The others – well, *¡qué vamos a hacer!*

105

Some of the young women and their children leave the procession to kiss Joan and me. We are touched by this display of affectionate family acceptance.

The procession gone by, the men make for the two bars, the women for home.

Tonight, as the rusty-faced church clock with its cracked voice chimes midnight, bands of youngsters will march through the village banging anything bangable, blowing horns and whistles, chanting, 'Rejoice all, *El Señor Jesus Cristo* is born.'

Why the ladies in white and black? Joan once asked Antonia and Pasión. Both looked at her as if she were mad. Why? Because that is the custom here. Always has been. It is what our ancestors did. It is what we do, and what those who come after us will do. What else?

I have asked our local priests. They do not know. In life we are in the midst of death, perhaps? A memento mori? But I must never forget that these villagers are *une gente rara*, a folk on their own, very strange, *muy aislada*, very isolated.

Other village processions are equally recondite. The Triumphal Entry into Jerusalem, for instance.

Paco Baker's little black donkey plays a central role. On the donkey's garment-covered back, Vitorio, fittingly enough our village carpenter, dressed as a black-bearded Jesus, rides with rejoicing gestures into the Holy City. Hosannas fill the air.

I smile at Joan. We are thinking the same thing.

Another donkey, black also but much, much bigger, in a remote village in the Alpujarras Altas, has been sacked this year for his libidinous behaviour. The owner of a herd of three cows complained to the mayor that Balzasar the donkey had attempted to violate each of his cows in turn.

Balzasar's owner, brought before the mayor and his officials, protested loudly that it was a plot hatched by the cows' proprietor, who by pure coincidence happened to have a suitable donkey to fulfil the honorific task.

The owner of the cows won the case hands down: Balzasar had been seen at his libidinous gambols by others in the village.

Even the inhabitants of so remote a village, it seems, were scandalised.

We look sympathetically at Paco's little care-worn donkey as he passes. We know, alas, that the wherewithal that might have tempted him to act like Balzasar had been sliced away early in his career. 'Trinklements', the St Ives word used in my boyhood for the whole apparatus, springs into my mind.

Pili, mistress of the bigger of the two village shops, heads the Good Friday procession. She is the possessor of a much-exercised superiority complex. In her clear powerful voice she is singing a mourning *saeta*. She holds her candle steady, shows no sign of emotion. The *saeta*? Spontaneous, no; memorised and well rehearsed, yes, but of unimpeachable sentiments.

Behind her walk Antonia and Pasión, both garbed in black. In one hand they carry lit candles; in the other a single trumpet lily, waxen white, its yellow stamen shocking in its bare boldness.

All the village widows follow, all in *luto*, the black they don when their husbands die and which they will be buried in. Each has a candle; many are tearful.

Cristo Himself is preceded by Paco Baker. He lugs across his shoulder the heavy wooden cross. The sweat from his huge balloon of a body mingles with his tears.

Next come the families. They are as silent as those ahead. The mothers have lit candles. Many are crying; many children also.

We wait for the procession to pass, then stroll down to the church, note the palms strewn in front of the door and wonder again where the women got them from.

We peer into the shadowy porch. Yes, there spread on the paving stones is the same large red cloak we have seen many times before, now much stained and trodden, but still serviceable. The Gospel story is followed to the letter, even though the chronology is somewhat shaky.

Another aspect of this foreignness, sun-drenched and so relaxed, is summed up in our villagers' complacent cheerful acknowledgement that we live in *el pais de mañana*, the country of tomorrow. The truth is, as they just as cheerfully agree when I put it to

107

them, that *nunca llega mañana en este pais*, tomorrow never comes in this country.

You cannot live at ease here among those Andalusians in our village unless you accept that they feel differently, think differently, do things differently.

You want a little job done? Good: the person you ask will come to do it *mañana*. He never turns up. You bump into him soon after. Why didn't he come? Oh, he forgot. Or he had something else to do. But he *will* come – *palabra*, promise – *mañana*!

No discernible sense of shame. No unease. No feeling that he has let you down. Yet he does not come tomorrow. He never comes. Thereafter when he meets you he behaves as he always has done, welcoming, friendly.

For a long time we found this hard to come to terms with. We were not helped by an experience which at the time we found as wounding as it was inexplicable.

We became firm friends with Antonio Casa, as we called the previous owner of our house, and his young and lively wife, Gador, and visited their house in the nearby recently-built settlement, the *urbanización*, a new house with none of the disadvantages of the old, Gador was quick to point out, and with much more life around them than in the village. We found Antonio's toothless mother quite a character, with the licensed tongue of old people, and spent enjoyable times on Antonio's land, never leaving without being laden with seasonal fruit, vegetables and salad.

Our nearby town had a very active *peña*, a club made up of lovers of flamenco – the genuine thing, of course, with the traditional *cante jondo*, profound song, of *saeta, soleás, siguiriyas, petenera*, and so on.

The club met monthly. When in funds, they invited one of the present-day masters of the art to come and give a performance. Following the custom at the *Feria de Sevilla*, only half-bottles of San Patricio were drunk: a sherry that if not drunk as soon as it was opened was not worth drinking at all, so they affirmed. And only on these occasions did the club barman produce the traditional *copitas*, the only fit glass for a fino.

We were delighted when Antonio asked us to be his guests to

hear the famous Fosforito, whose tapes I had much enjoyed. 'I and my woman will come for you at ten o'clock. ¿*De acuerdo?* Plenty of time to get to the *peña* and drink a *copita* before it begins.'

We ate our usual leisurely dinner at 7.30, dressed up for the occasion, and sat down full of anticipation to wait for the arrival of Antonio and Gador.

We went on waiting. No Antonio. No word. Perhaps I had mistaken the time? Eleven o'clock, not ten?

Time dragged on. At 11.30 we became really anxious. What could have happened? Someone taken ill? An accident? We sincerely hoped not. But . . . ?

We finally went puzzled to bed, still anxious. It must be something serious, surely?

And what in fact had happened? Antonio was a member of what was the equivalent of our parish council. The chairman had suddenly decided to call a meeting the evening of the *peña* visit. He had contacted Antonio and other members that afternoon.

Doubtless, Antonio felt he had to put duty before pleasure. Fair enough, I suppose – but he had ample time to let us know. An intelligent young man, who had read some of the major poets, who was well able to discuss politics and world affairs, it never entered his head to let us know. Neither did it Gador's.

Nor, when we met him and heard what he had to say, did he feel the need to apologise: how could he when he had behaved as he normally would with friends on such occasions?

End of friendship.

In view of all this, and of the times we were invited to a village for an evening drink, only to find the wife had not been told and that the host [*sic*] turned up much later, I having sweated blood to try and keep some sort of conversation going, we decided on the only possible stance to take. However alike on the surface they and we appeared to be, however friendly and generous and likeable they were, we should never forget that under the skin they were different, alien, fickle as children, and as forgetful.

Soon after the Antonio Casa incident, Felix, by far the most intellectual of our three padre acquaintances (I use the word advisedly) said something to us which threw some light on the situation we found ourselves in:

'I divide people into three classes. One, brothers. You are blessed if in this life you find any of these. Two, friends. They are rare. If you find them, cling to them. My race, unfortunately, has in my opinion little capacity for friendship. Three, acquaintances. And what is there to be said about acquaintances?'

We resolved then and there we should in future regard everybody here as merely acquaintances. Not get involved. Enjoy to the full their openness, their sun-drenched happy-go-lucky attitude, their childlike spontaneity, their generosity. But remember always that they like to be liked, that they want to be accepted for what they are by these fortunate foreigners – as their equals! – that the efforts they accordingly make can easily be mistaken for what we conceive of as friendship.

A very necessary self-denying ordinance for me, far more susceptible to people than Joan, far more drawn to them, far more inclined to see friendship where there is none, far more inclined to believe in humanity in general.

Life in the village goes its unvarying, seasonal, peaceful way. Yet violence – lethal violence – is liable to erupt at any time.

The 1936–39 Civil War, still ever present in the folk memory, made members of the same family, here and throughout Spain, slaughter each other. Our village, except for a small minority of its inhabitants, was solidly Republican, bitterly anti-Franco. The old people still recall Franco's German and Italian allies swarming over the hills, occupying the area, and the hunger and hardship they suffered.

Franco wreaked his revenge on them after his victory, cutting off the water from the Sierra Nevada that fed their irrigation channels. Result: they could grow little, and what they could grow was poor – *papas*, potatoes, for instance, as small as marbles.

When Franco believed he had taught them their lesson, he gave the village the land now occupied by Calle Cruces. We derive considerable satisfaction from the fact that we are enjoying part of what was once his: Franco our benefactor.

There are two poets whose names at least are familiar to everyone here: Juan Ramón Jiménez and Federico García Lorca.

Lorca's 'The Unfaithful Married Woman' is perhaps the best-known poem in modern Spanish literature, a poem known by heart by some of the older men who cannot read.

The universal opinion of young men and old was that if their wives were unfaithful, they would kill them.

I did not take this seriously: they are all great bar talkers. How wrong I was.

It happened one quiet spring day, the men in the fields, the women preparing the *almuerzo*, the main two o'clock meal, the children home from school and waiting to be fed before going back at three o'clock.

The two gunshots from somewhere near the church shattered the silence. Only later did we learn that the *alcalde*, the village mayor, a big, beefy, bald, jovial man in his early forties, with three lovely children, two girls and a boy, had murdered his wife after locking the children in the bedroom.

Reason? He was convinced his wife was having an affair with his brother . . . And was she? No one was prepared to say then; no one has been prepared to say since.

For many years we were the only foreigners living in the village. Then the stranger arrived, causing as much stir as we did when we first came.

No one knew his nationality or where he came from. The girl he brought with him could speak nothing but Italian, or to be more precise the Neapolitan dialect, which I knew well enough to identify.

Despite the great disparity in their age, we took them for man and wife. Our neighbour Isabel soon disillusioned us. They were only a *pareja*, pair, not a *matrimonio*, married couple. 'Who,' she said, 'can respect a pair, especially when the male is so much older, the female fit to be his daughter, not his woman.'

The couple lodged with the man we called Juan Bible, a most devout Catholic, one of only two men in the village who attended mass. He had room to spare, his two eldest daughters were married and only his youngest, Teresa, was still at home.

I met the stranger in Antonio's bar opposite the church. It was a Sunday evening and the bar was busy. I found myself standing next to the stranger at the counter, but he appeared not to notice me. A tall thin man of about 50, he had long greying hair, a Zapata moustache, a pearl in the lobe of his left ear. The thick pebbled spectacles he wore made it impossible to see his eyes.

Juan Bible, a man not easily impressed, already seemed to be hanging on his every word.

Juan introduced me. '*Enchanté, m'sieur*,' the stranger said, offering his hand in a lordly gesture.

'*Tanto gusto, señor*,' I replied.

He ignored my Spanish and kept on speaking in French.

Extremely courteous and affable, I knew instinctively this was not the real man. He was only putting on a show for the benefit of Juan and the others now crowding the counter, watching and listening with their usual childlike curiosity.

Tired of his little game, I began to speak French also. 'Staying long?' I said, surprised to find myself fervently hoping he was only passing through.

He said he was a businessman and intended to live here – in his own house, of course. He pressed his big spectacles back onto the bridge of his long hooked nose with a nicotine-stained forefinger.

I waited for him to tell me what his business was, but waited in vain.

Later I asked myself why I had bothered with a man I disliked so. Was it simply pride? Did I simply want to show the villagers I could hold my own with him in French? Was it that he was already figuring as a person of some importance in their eyes?

I was confirmed in this suspicion when Roberto, as I now knew him to be, insisted on buying drinks for his host and those standing near him.

To my utter astonishment, they accepted. The unwritten rule here was that no one not of the village was allowed to buy a drink. When a visitor wanted to pay, he found he owed nothing: the man who had nodded to the barman each time the visitor ordered a drink would settle after the visitor had gone.

112

Early on in my time in the village, I had tried to stand my round, or at least pay for my own drink. Nothing doing; the barman would refuse to take my money. So unsatisfactory did I find this that I soon stopped going regularly to the bars. The only way I could have paid was to have quarrelled with my neighbours.

What an impression this newcomer must have made on them. They had obviously decided he was a man of substance, judging him by his superior airs, the way he dressed – embroidered waistcoat over silk shirt, black leather pants, tooled Mexican boots – and by the fact (to be surreptitiously envied?) that he had so young and desirable a partner with him?

Teresa came into the bar to fetch her father and his guest; supper was ready.

All the men, even the noisy card players, fell momentarily silent. Can you wonder? Here was a 16-year-old in full flower. It was as if she were new minted. She shone: eyes, skin, teeth, hair. We were all caught by her beauty, her slumbering sexuality. Yet such appeared to be her innocence she seemed quite unaware of the effect she had on us.

But was she really so innocent? Neighbour Isabel was completely certain she was.

'Yes, Alberto, yes, she *is* innocent. Not for Teresa the accompanied walk through the flowering canes to the river bank where it is well known what happens, though no one ever speaks about it. Teresa, Teresa, I swear on my life, is as innocent as orange blossom.'

I did not feast my eyes on Teresa when she came into the bar; I kept them on Roberto. He had drawn himself up to his full height as she entered. Now he stepped forward, took Teresa's hand, bent over and kissed it. If my looks could have killed he would have been dead there and then.

I expected Juan to show unease; hand kissing is not something we go in for here. But no. He seemed flattered. And, reluctant as I was to admit it, so did Teresa.

Even when he held her hand a moment longer than was strictly necessary, she made no attempt to withdraw it. But, then, why should she, naïve as she was?

I turned to the doorway to see what effect this was having on

113

the lad standing there watching. Nico was now 18. A bit soft in the head, that was how they expressed it tolerantly, smilingly. When his father died, his mother was left with six children to rear. Juan Bible was her next-door neighbour; he as good as adopted Nico and brought him up as one of his own children, apart from the fact he never slept in Juan's house.

We had watched Nico growing up with Teresa, and I confess we foresaw problems. A nice enough lad, his childishness could at times be endearing. The older he grew, though, the more dependent on Teresa he became. This last year or so, it became obvious to me he was beginning to regard her as something more than a sister.

What exactly took place we never found out. Two months ago Juan had suddenly turned Nico out of the house.

No one saw him for a fortnight. From the moment he reappeared, he became Teresa's shadow. That it had been a traumatic experience for him was proved by what his poor mother told us.

'For fifteen days my Nico would not leave the house. Hardly ate anything . . . I know he is not like others, but he was a loving son . . . Now he is utterly changed. Will not even speak to me, his mother, any more.'

'But he still works?'

'*Gracias a Dios, sí.* He is the eldest. A man now, he must work to keep bread in the mouths of the little ones. Francisco and I work also, but that is not enough.'

'And how does he pass his time when he is not working?'

'He stays waiting for Teresa to come out. Follows her like a dog. Never near enough, *gracias a Dios*, to cause her distress.'

I put my fears to Fausto, the old padre who occasionally stood in for Padre Ramón. Fausto did not think my fears well grounded. Why? Because he had noted where Nico sat at mass: always where he could see Teresa's face. 'For Nico, it is not the Virgin who is sacred, it is Teresa. And if you could see the love on his face, you would know he could not harm her.'

When Roberto kissed Teresa's hand and held it for that moment longer than was necessary, I saw by the look on Nico's face that, simple as he was, he had got the message just as clearly as I had.

114

I wondered apprehensively how he would react. I was very relieved when he turned on his heel and disappeared . . .

It was Isabel who as usual told us the news.

'Roberto has bought Juan's house.'

'In the *plaza*?'

'No, of course not. What would Juan do without a house? The other one. It has been empty since his mother died. It has been empty long enough. Such houses as ours need to be lived in.'

The house was in a bad state of repair, as Isabel had implied. Roberto and his woman moved in right away. They made do with what they found there – nothing had been touched since Juan's mother died.

Soon two Germans, a mason and a carpenter, arrived in a clapped-out van. They quickly put the house to rights, going into town to bring back new furniture, bed linen, utensils, a fridge – yes, a fridge!

The villagers were more impressed than ever. A man of substance, indeed. Those who were his neighbours were pleased to say so; it increased their prestige in the eyes of the others.

The Germans, I was very sorry to see, stayed on. There was plenty of work for them. They also did not mind working in the fields when work was slack.

Soon a shrivelled-up Spaniard, not an Andalusian, a perpetual talker, arrived and took up residence in Roberto's house. In the bars, in his rusty drink-sodden voice, he boasted he was a great friend of don Roberto's. No one was fooled; he was in fact Roberto's servant.

'What number of visitors the stranger has,' Isabel informed us, not bothering to hide her disapproval. 'What hospitality he offers. What money he must have.'

This, together with the fact that Roberto would often go off for days on end in his ancient Mercedes, led the villagers to conclude he was a *contrabandista*, smuggler, which added further to his standing.

This conclusion became a certainty when the Guardia Civil

came one afternoon during siesta and arrested a man who had arrived that very morning at Roberto's.

'He had killed another man,' said Isabel with great satisfaction. Demonstrated with equal relish how the Guardia had handcuffed the murderer. Bustled him into their car and driven away.

Like many older people, she credited the Guardia with almost supernatural powers. They alone, now that Generalísimo Franco was dead, stood between us and chaos – robbery, murder, rape, and heaven knows what else.

Did all this put Roberto in bad odour with the village men? On the contrary. In Antonio's bar, he was now more than ever the centre of admiring attention.

Juan Bible, though, being such a devout Catholic, would surely distance himself, fight shy of him?

I was wrong. Every Sunday evening after six o'clock mass, Juan would be at Roberto's side, hardly sparing a word for me, staring at Roberto, listening to him as if he were the Pope himself.

One morning – I suppose it must have been about three months after Roberto's arrival – Isabel brought us some tomatoes. Hardly had she handed them over than out she came with it.

'The Germans have gone. Gone for ever.' Here she paused to take a deep breath. 'And Roberto's woman, she has gone with them.' Another dramatic pause. 'At least she and he must have been lovers, old though he is. But the Germans. What can she be to the Germans?'

We could see from the look on her face that she had not finished yet.

'You know,' she said, 'Roberto has many guests?' She did not wait for a reply. 'Now that his woman has gone, Juan has agreed that Teresa can go to help him. He cannot look after them himself, of course.'

'But his man, the Spaniard, why can't he –'

'He is a nothing. A drunkard. How can he be trusted to treat the guests with respect? Serve at table?'

Her news disturbed me more than I cared to admit. 'And what is your opinion of this?'

Isabel shrugged, raised her hands, palm upwards, the sign here that no responsibility is accepted. 'What should my opinion be? It is her father's wish. That is his right.'

She did, however, permit herself one observation. 'You understand, if her mother was alive, Teresa would be too busy at home sewing and crocheting the things she would need when she married to spend time as a servant in a stranger's house.'

'Why isn't she doing that?'

'Her father has no plans for her marriage, so his sister told me. Not for a long time.'

The mention of marriage brought Nico to mind. 'And Nico? What news is there of Nico? I haven't seen him about lately.'

Isabel shrugged again. 'Nico? When Teresa is in Roberto's house, Nico takes the goats. He goes and sits on the hill behind the house, waits and watches until Teresa goes into her own house.'

They found her among the reeds, where, according to Isabel, she never voluntarily went. She was naked. Her face was discoloured. Her tongue protruded. Her legs were spread wide. Between her breasts a cross fashioned from the leaves of the reeds had been carefully placed.

There had been a savage and prolonged struggle – of this the smashed and trampled reeds gave clear evidence.

They did not touch her. They left her lying as they had found her. Immediately summoned her father.

One look and Juan turned away. He knew who her killer was. Only one person had from time to time these last few weeks fashioned such crosses and offered them to his daughter.

He crossed himself. 'Life for life. So says the Sacred Bible. Amen.'

Without another word, another look back at his daughter, Juan strode away.

They found Nico the next day in the same spot as they had found Teresa. He had been stripped, horribly mutilated. The wounds that finally finished him off were two deep gashes exactly where the reed cross had been placed between his daughter's breasts.

117

The Guardia Civil came the same day to take Juan away. After they handcuffed him, they showed him the broken spectacles with the thick pebbled lenses they had found among the trampled reeds.

No need for words. They had to support Juan as the full horror of the mistake he had made dawned on him.

'Roberto,' he moaned. 'Where is Roberto?'

'Gone.'

Still dazed, Juan stuttered. 'Go – gone? B-but where?'

'Who can tell? But rest assured. Without any doubt whatsoever we shall find him.'

They never did.

We witnessed Nico's funeral. No black solemn lines. Only men in working clothes walk casually as if coming home from the fields. They are silent, their eyes attentive, their gaze on the shouldered coffin that leads them from Nico's house to the church. The women wait in the church.

Now also a little girl is being interred. The coffin is minute and all white, held at waist level by four teenage girls. The girls following are brightly dressed, silent, hands filled with flowers, faces triumphant.

From the red-brick tower of *La Iglesia de Nuestra Virgin de las Angustias*, the colour of ancient dried blood, at five in the afternoon the passing bells toll for the mourning mass.

The bones, the bones are left for veneration when the body, God's image, dissolves into dust.

The sound of the bells in our lonely valley sprinkles the village with tarnished silver and bronze.

The bones, the bones are left for veneration when the body, created in God's image, dissolves into dust.

The high silver voice of the little bell draws up to heaven the abiding memories of the fortunate faithful, awakens in their soul images of their lost ones, colour of dust-laden silver.

The bones, the bones are left for veneration when the body, created in God's image, dissolves into dust.

The deep bronze voice of the big bell, in the hearts of the

118

unfaithful summons back their ghosts, already almost forgotten, sullied profiles, shadowy sad shapes, silver-verdigris colour.

The bones, the bones are left for veneration when the body, created in God's image, dissolves into dust.

14

The man, more scarecrow than man, we call CWV, the Civil War Veteran, is one of the few who did not hasten to retire when they became of pensionable age. Now in his eighties, he has not handed over his land to his sons.

Three of his choicest *parcelas*, each a prime site, lie on the edge of the village. There you can see him doing little or nothing, but directing his two large long-suffering sons on what work to do next, and how to do it.

These two, now in their forties, sleek and unlined, as unlike their little, wizened father as they could possibly be, take it all in good part, show not the least sign of impatience. After all, surely their father, he who has so many years on his shoulders, will soon be laid to rest – ¡*qué desanse en paz*!, may he rest in peace – with his ancestors, then they can work the land, their land it will be. No sister to share it with. Their only sister is dead – ¡*qué descanse en paz también*!

We now try to avoid the CWV. Not because we do not like him – we do – but because he insists on recounting the same tale about his deeds in the Civil War. His hatred of Franco and his German and Italian allies is as alive, as powerful, today as it was in 1936 when he joined the Republicans as a boy of 13; at least that is what he says was his age.

Bleary-eyed, his thin lips as they move revealing an all but toothless mouth, he talks in his thin, trembly voice about the various campaigns he took part in. Always, though, he comes back to the Battle of Teruel that raged from December 1937 to February 1938 on the southern Aragon front.

His abiding memory is not of the final disastrous defeat of the

120

Republican army, with 20,000 dead and many more wounded and taken prisoner, but of the terrible, unbelievable cold. Temperatures fell to as low as 18 degrees below zero, and many fighters on both sides suffered from severe frostbite. Slaughter and suffering, yes. But such cold experienced by a south coast Andalusian born and bred – impossible!

From Teruel, the C W V returned to his own village, and when we first heard this part of his story, we were amazed.

'I was a Republican. Still am. Never will I change, never. See those old men standing over there? Those are two who learned nothing from the Civil War. They still say, "We lived better under Franco", ignoring the innocent people he had killed, the jails filled with innocent people, their only offence that they spoke out against him.'

The C W V spat to show his contempt.

'And see that man standing over there, taking the sun in front of his shop? Look at him while I spit again . . . That man was the village informer. Now he prospers. That man, *maldita sea*, may he be damned, was responsible for the death of so many here in my village, my own brother among them. My sister's man, my two nephews also. Sold to Franco's men for thirty pieces of silver.'

He closed his eyes for a moment before going on.

'I well remember these hills alive with soldiers, Germans, Italians, Franco's hired brutes with their modern weapons. And we, men and boys, armed with knives, axes, spades, sticks, stones, anything. The mayor himself, he who lives in the grand house in the village square, that man, believe me, friend, sold his own brother. Franco's men shot him. I saw it with my own eyes.'

The C W V wiped his own watering eyes with the back of one grimy hand.

'The worst, for there are many worse things than a clean death, was to come. Soldiers took our food, our crops, our livestock. The old people died of hunger. And who could bear to hear the children crying, their mothers as well? Not I. I made up my mind to fight, go and join those the church called Godless rebels, Godless Reds. And I *did* fight. Fought till we were defeated. Our own fault; we could not agree, were more keen to fight among ourselves than against Franco's men.'

The CWV wiped the spittle from his trembling lips; I thought they looked even more livid than usual.

'The traitors here prosper now, as in all Spain – the Church saw to that. And I, I am poor, but I have no regrets. Right is right. With clear conscience, I sleep soundly at night ... But how do traitors, murderers, sleep?'

The CWV's admiration for his relative Elena, *La Soltera*, The Spinster, is unbounded. We were not surprised she was a relative: all the villagers seem related to each other. Certainly they are always eager to point out proudly when someone is mentioned that they are *familia*.

'Elena,' the CWV was never tired of saying, 'a woman as good as any man when she was young ... And why did she not marry? Because all the young men were afraid of her, a woman who wore a pistol on her hip, who worked alone on her land.'

Elena. Unmarried daughters. Their lot, as *El Bicicletista* averred, was mostly an unhappy one.

Soon after I had begun studying flamenco, using tapes of some famous *cantaores* such as Antonio Moreno, Sabicas, Maña Vargus and Fosforito, young Eduardo who lived in Calle Principal invited us to the *matanza* in his uncle's *cortijo* up in the hills.

Enough was enough. I was about to make some excuse when he said, 'My uncle still has fame in the region as a singer of *cante jondo*, profound song. None of your false flamenco they perform on the coast for the tourists. You wish, Alberto, to become an *aficionado* of the art? Then come and hear my uncle. A chance not to be missed.'

I was consequently glad to accept.

The *cortijo* was much grander than we had expected, the second-day *matanza* feast the most lavish we had so far attended. The barbecued pork in particular was a gourmet treat. The wine, at least the wine our host served himself and me with – Joan refused – was a complete surprise, quite unlike any mountain wine I had drunk.

My host proudly told me what it was. A *rancio*, 15 years old, from the big bodega in Albondón. Very dear, but worth it, did I not agree?

I *did* agree. A wine with sherry overtones. Reminiscent of a good dry oloroso (there are no sweet sherries in Spain, a contradiction in terms).

A real find, this *rancio*. Highly alcoholic; I could already feel it. No matter: Joan drove these mountain roads superbly.

Our host Manuel's four daughters were present. The three married bustled animatedly about, leaving their mother nothing to do but keep a general eye. The youngest, Mari Guadalupe, by far the prettiest, shy, subdued, at everyone's beck and call, took no part in the conversation. She was too occupied with all the menial tasks to have any time to spare to socialise, even if she had wanted to: a veritable Cinderella.

The feast finished, Manuel fetched his guitar and gave it to one of his sons-in-law. Everybody settled down, the men by now utterly relaxed.

Manuel waited for absolute silence. He seemed to grow taller before my very eyes. A fine, handsome man, his dark eyes shone. So did his black carefully brushed and lacquered hair. He briefly touched his eyebrow-thin jet-black moustache, lifted his head, drew in a deep breath.

I looked for Mari Guadalupe. She had disappeared. To do what menial tasks, I wondered? And I thought of what *El Bicicletista* had once said to me about the lot of unmarried girls.

Foot on a stool, the guitarist struck a few *rasgueos*, the flourishes quiet at first, then becoming louder and louder.

A sudden dramatic pause. As Manuel began to sing his *coplas*, his verses, eyes closed, expression infinitely sad, his other sons-in-law began the rhythmic clapping, the *palmas*.

This was *cante jondo* I was being privileged to hear, *solea, siguiriya, petenera* following each other. Tears ran down the *cantaor*'s face as he sang.

The recital ended. Manuel smilingly and unabashed wiped away the tears. No one moved; no one spoke. The listeners, I concluded, were as moved as he was.

The spell was finally broken by Mari Guadalupe bringing in the coffee.

Later that evening at home, I reread what Lorca himself said about *cante jondo*: 'Millenarian, mysterious, oriental, spiritual, pantheistic, ritualised, its atavistic, pagan world has no morning nor evening, no mountains nor plains. It consists solely of the blue night of Andalusia, wide and deeply starred. The chief protagonist is the woman, always *morena*, dark, possessor of the "rose". She is called *Pena*, pain, agony, suffering, love made flesh. Ever present by her side is Death himself. The guitar follows the singer and the songs' undulating rhythms. Its occasional *falseta*, flourish, is the commentary made by the strings on the words. The singing is often a trilling, imitating birdsong, animal cries, the sounds of nature. Often the same note is repeated, as in certain forms of magic, and of ancient pagan and church rituals. There are links with Indian, Moorish, Byzantine and Jewish music, and with the music still heard in Morocco and Tunisia today'.

And what is the ideal setting in which to hear *cante jondo*? The poet Luis Rosales, Lorca's friend and 12 years his junior, gives the answer: 'For *cante jondo* to pain us, strike us, it must be heard by a circle of friends in a reserved room in a tavern, among the smoke, the sadness, the wine. To the Andaluz, the sound of the guitar is the epitome of sorrow and pity. There is no sound like it. Its black sounds have been dying for centuries'.

It was these 'black sounds' that were Lorca's inspiration. For him they were the spirit of the earth of his native Andalusia.

In his book of poems, *Poema del cante jondo*, Lorca personifies each *cante jondo* form as a woman. In his group of poems about each, he expresses what his feelings and reactions were as he listened. His profound understanding of these flamenco forms, which he had been steeped in as a child, enabled him to delve into the very heart and soul of each.

*   *   *

The only name this white-haired little man has in the village is *El Cantaor*, the Flamenco Singer. No one knows where he came from, though some believe it was Cádiz, the home of all the true flamenco singers.

He practically lives in Pedro's bar, our largest and cleanest. The villagers are unfailingly kind to him. Stand him drinks when he is out of funds. No need to ask what he wants. Cognac – the name they still use, though now forbidden by law, the French producers having won their battle in the courts to have the name banned in Spain – was his only drink, what he would seemingly spend all his money on.

They would wait unsmiling for his performance when he had drunk enough.

Livid face, rheumy eyes, you gulp another brandy, raise your rusty voice.

The *siguiriya* you sing resurrects – true *gitano* born and bred – the famed flamenco singer you were, banishes for a moment the burden of your unending debauchery, promise unfulfilled, hope long since dissipated, an unbounded future unrealised.

Today, brandy is for you roof and walls, hearth and heat, sleep and sustenance, work and rest, wife and children, sunrise and sunset, sunshine and shade.

The *siguiriya* ends. Only indifferent silence surrounds you, broken at last by someone murmuring, perhaps in jest, *Olé*. Yet your ears are filled by the sounds of long ago, the prolonged plaudits of your audience, and you cannot hide your tears.

At last you swill another brandy and, wounded beast, you go stumbling away on the stony track that leads to your cheerless hovel.

The bodega at Albodón had huge high-roofed caverns, cool and damp, linked one to another. All contained enormous oak barrels, two or three times my height, and the inner cavern contained the *rancio*.

The minimum purchase was five litres ... How much did I want? Five, ten, sixteen? Two *garrafas* of five? Good: here was a serious customer ... And the age? Anything from 15 years to

30. And there was still some 40-year-old left, if . . . But take care – any wine older than 15 would *cuesta un ojo*, cost an eye.

I asked the prices per litre, more out of banal curiosity than anything else, and hid my astonishment as best I could at the cost of the older. I hastily settled for the 15-year-old; that was quite dear enough for me.

Now for the tasting. The cellarman climbed the ladder. Dipped in the long, slim rod with the silver thimble-cup at the end. Climbed slowly down. Poured the wine into my rinsed, cold glass. Ordered me to smell before sniffing. And to hold the wine against my palate before swallowing.

Tastings from three more barrels of 15-year-old. I made a show of debating with myself under his scrutiny, then chose the last, guessing he would have kept the best till then.

He nodded his approval. Assured me I had a good palate. Insisted on carrying the two 5-litre *garrafas* to the office, where I paid.

Had I deceived myself, I wondered as we drove down the steep winding road that led to the coast? Had I wasted good money? Trying to recapture something of an experience in Manuel's *cortijo* which, by its very nature, was unique?

Fortunately, no. The *rancio* drank as well as I had hoped, both as aperitif, and after dinner when we were reading and listening to music.

The Cinderella story had a happy ending.

Two years later, we were invited to her wedding, a grand affair by village standards: was not the father a proud man, a man of substance as well as a famed *cantaor* with a reputation to maintain?

At the reception, we asked ourselves if this flushed, animated girl could really be Cinderella. No one could wish to see a lovelier bride.

And when I went to hold her hand and kiss her, to wish her all good fortune, she radiated such virginal heat that I involuntarily glanced with surmise at the young man who had just become her lucky husband. With also the faintest suspicion of envy, if the truth be told.

This question of daughters marrying. A father's view, to put it crudely, is that his girls should repay him for their upbringing, take their share of work on the land until he, their father, decides the time has come to let them go. Despite men and women alike proclaiming that the woman rules the house, in this matter she has no voice whatsoever: what the husband says, goes. It is right and proper for the daughter to have a *novio*, a fiancé – indeed it would be regarded as a slight if she did not – but it would be years before they could marry.

Knowing this, when I ask them when are they going to marry, they put a good face on it, smile, shrug, say they do not know yet, there is plenty of time. The more thoughtful add that they and their *novio* must get enough money together first.

Girls flower young in this climate. To be forced by their father to wait years and years when each long day the call of the wild becomes stronger, ever more urgent, is a real pain.

Some have found a way out.

The first time I heard of this, I was a bit shocked. Among these staunch Catholics (the women certainly are), being a virgin was something a girl took into her marriage, a gift to her husband. But this particular 16-year-old – yes, only 16 – had got herself pregnant and been hastily taken to the altar. Not a shotgun wedding, of course: the groom was as eager as was his bride.

It was the old *cura*, Fausto, who performed the ceremony. He smiled beatifically when I asked him about it.

'The flesh, as you know, Alberto, is weak. And who among us is fit to be judge? The young people are married now. In *La Iglesia de Nuestra Virgin de las Angustias*, where she was baptised and has been a faithful attender at mass ... I agree they are mere children. They will have their problems. But with the help of *El Señor*, they will overcome them. What can we do but wish them well? I look forward to baptising their first child here in our village church into the true faith.'

I already knew Fausto was philosopher as well as priest. He

had served his church for many years in Calcutta, which was where he had picked up his delightfully quaint English accent and Victorian turn of speech.

I remembered when we took him a selection of choice teas and a fine china teapot. Such teas were not at that time readily available in our region; and if they had been, they would have been too dear for his pocket.

His pleasure was a rich reward. 'All those years in Calcutta, Juanita, believe me, I drank only tea made from the dust of the leaves. And now . . . four kinds of the finest English teas. Wait until I show Padres Felix and Ramón how to make real tea in a china pot.'

Fausto often dwelt on the poverty he had witnessed in Calcutta, the dead and dying bodies you had to step over as you went along.

I shuddered, blessed my good sense in turning down some years ago the offer by the British Council to become their man in Calcutta, though they had warned me of the inevitable culture shock if I took the job.

Piles of dead and dying bodies. Women and children starving daily to death. When I asked Fausto how he had coped, I shall never forget his reply, nor the angelic untroubled smile he accompanied it with.

'Simple, Alberto. As a man of God and a Catholic, I was concerned only with their souls, not their bodies.'

It was Ramón. *el tonto*, the daft one, Fausto called him, who put the china teapot on the gas ring – end of teapot

The 16-year-old girl seemed to have set a precedent. The next to get herself put in the family way was the pretty, pert little daughter of the local carpenter, Vitoriano. Maria, his wife, a regular goer to mass who took turns with Pili to head the Easter procession following *La Virgen de Neustras Angustias* as she was carried through the village.

Maria, candle in hand, like Pili, led the singing, rendering her own idea of a *saeta*, a palid imitation, but most sincere, nevertheless.

A dyed blonde, she certainly gave herself airs, taking pains to moderate her accent, to talk slowly, when she was speaking to *lawingléh*, as if we were not all there.

When the news got about that her pampered daughter Rocío, the Spanish word for 'dew', was pregnant, Maria showed her the door. Like Niobe, she dissolved into tears whenever some woman expressed her sympathy. Lamented her betrayal. Vowed that not a thing would the daughter have, not one thing. Vitoriano? Vitoriano agreed with her, of course. Was he not as hurt as she was?

Rocío had gone to live with her fiancé's parents. She got married elsewhere, none of her own family being invited. What a disgrace. How sad.

Not a bit of it. As soon as the baby arrived, all was forgiven. The village house Rocío's parents then gave her had been gutted, done up outside and in, and was now the most modern by far in the village. As good, in fact, as those chalets away over the hill where the foreigners lived.

Vitoriano himself, aided by good friends of his, a mason, a plumber, an electrician, had worked like demons, a quite unheard of thing here.

The whole of the façade was tiled, the pattern striking, if somewhat bizarre. This, added to the new glass-panelled door, windows and fancy scrolled grey-painted *rejas*, ensured the house was as unlike any other village house as possible. Inside also (to coin a phrase) there was every modern convenience.

What a house this was. How it put the house of *lawingléh* in its place – a house that was still a village house, so far as they could see, with no modern conveniences whatsoever, except for the *cuarto de baño*.

The new family moved in. Granny Maria immediately took over the baby, a bright-eyed, jet-black curly-haired little girl who doubtless reminded her of her errant daughter when she was a baby.

Rocío ran the shop, while Granny, *la abuela*, displayed her grandchild to the customers. The boyish husband had by now qualified as a teacher, a prestigious fact. He was not of the village, which perhaps accounted for his hasty ways, so my neighbour, Isabel, thought, conveniently ignoring the precedent set by the local lad.

The young husband, alas, had no permanent post. He did earn

something, however, *dando clases*, giving private lessons, in mathematics in the nearby town. But with in-laws like his, why should he worry? As it was, there was always something for him to do concerned with the shop.

The ruse caught on. No father could refuse to allow his daughter to marry and face having her bring a *bastardo* into the world: the disgrace would be intolerable.

Nevertheless, I was still slightly shocked when two lovely girls we knew well, one the daughter of our lemons-for-marmalade supplier, the other, one of the daughters of Maria M3D, Mother of Three Daughters, as we had named her at once when we found her family and ours matched exactly.

Result – both girls quickly married without any false fuss by their parents; both went off to live in little modern duplex houses in one of the new *urbanizaciónes* where only young couples like themselves lived (what a change for the better).

They visited their parents regularly, brought in due course their babies to be fussed over and left with *la abuela* when it suited. And *los abuelos*? Never, even in this village, were there more doting grandparents.

Eloise and Antonio were our next-door neighbours. They had two teenage daughters, smooth and sleek as seals. Eloise in her mid-thirties was also blessed with an abundance of lovely flesh; black hair, brown eyes, strikingly white teeth shone in an untroubled and attractive round face.

When she brought her newly-born tail-ender in for us to see, I turned in astonishment to Joan.

'Did you know she was pregnant?'

'Of course! Where are your eyes?'

My eyes, I assured her, were where they had always been, yet I had never noticed a single extra inch added to our neighbour's ample bow-windowed front.

Eloise was smiling broadly, and looked in her twenties. '*Es un macho, Juanita, ¡es un macho!*' she exclaimed as she handed the rounded, dark, curly-haired little boy to Joan.

We fussed over the baby, were sincerely pleased that this 'gift from God' was a boy, here in this area where males are still all that count.

During the first two years of young Antonito's life, he was never left alone for a single minute. When mother and daughters went into the fields, the *bisabuela*, the great-grandmother, now over 90 and still able to sew and crochet without glasses, would come creaking, bent almost double, one hand on hip, the other clutching a stick as gnarled as herself, to sit by the baby's cot. Her tiny dark eyes would be fixed on her precious Antonito: nothing, but nothing, was going to happen to him if she could help it. From her sentinel position she never stirred until Isabel returned from work.

You can imagine what a spoiled and overprotected little lad we saw growing up. He got his own way in everything, especially in not going to school. His method was simple, but extremely effective: he'd walk a few yards from his front door, lie down in the dust, kick his heels hard enough to raise a little yellow cloud, and yell loud enough to bring the women to their doors. After a brief interval, Eloise would appear and beckon him back indoors. Nevertheless, Antonito is now a well-behaved, courteous, helpful and manly lad who goes without complaint to the secondary school in the nearby town. At weekends, he goes equally willingly into the fields to work alongside his family, something he resolutely refused to do in those early years.

Eloise's sister, now nearing 30, has Down's syndrome. She is, as the old *bisabuela* avers, a special gift from God.

She lives with her parents. Her father, good-natured but too fond of lifting his elbow, is nicknamed *El Corcho*, The Cork. He looks after a huge stand of orange groves on the flat land skirting the coast and some distance from the village. The house goes with the job. The two rich brothers who own the groves trust *El Corcho* implicitly and visit but rarely, but always at the *matanza*.

As the dear neighbours of Eloise, we have a permanent invitation to visit Casabella. We go during the orange season. We know we will come away with sacks of whatever kind of orange we fancy. This always includes a special kind of tangerine, Joan's favourite.

131

Part of our reason for going is to smell the orange blossom and the lemon blossom as we wander through the orchard. We are transported. Little wonder orange blossom is thought to bring such blessings at weddings here: the fragrance, the fragrance!

Eloisita, the Down's syndrome daughter, is always waiting at the door to greet us. We accept (how could we refuse?) her wet and slobbery kisses, avoiding when we are quick, their landing affectionately on our lips.

As often as not, her mother excuses her man; he is having a siesta after a hard morning's work. She invites us in, offers me a glass of raw mountain *mosto* (grape juice), which I refuse, then suggests we go to the *naranjal* to pick what we want.

Usually, *El Corcho* joins us in the grove, still very unsteady on his pins, but voicing his great pleasure at seeing us. He urges his wife and us to pick, pick, pick. Tries to help and becomes entangled in the branches.

Back in the house, coffee for Joan (decaffeinated. which she hates), wine poured by *El Corcho* with much spilling for me and him. The tapas are delicious; fresh crusty bread, ham from their own pig, and black olives.

Eloisita sits silent, smiles contentedly at us. Grossly over-weight, we know that eating is her great pleasure, yet she does not reach out to the big plate of tapas.

As we drive home, we discuss once again the practice the state adopts down here of paying parents enough and to spare to care for such handicapped progeny as Eloisita at home. Certainly much cheaper than any system we know of. Better? Well, Eloisita is well-behaved, well-mannered, and seems happy and contented, untroubled as she was by being sent to school when she was of school age. Her parents did not think it necessary. Of course she is still never allowed out on her own.

15

The small cart stationary at the edge of the market is weighed down by the load it contains. Five children at the front, one boy, four girls – bad luck here where boys mean so much – their faces brown as their donkey's coat, squash good-humouredly against each other.

Their donkey, also small and fat, swells most contentedly to fill the space between the slender shafts, stands motionless and dozing in the midday sun.

The mother lies in the shade of the painted hood, some of the paint long since faded from the canvas. Her breast yields to tiny fingers, while a determined mouth pulls at the teat and bubbles white. Children and mother meet my glance, smile instantly, teeth whiter than the bubbling milk. Father is nowhere to be seen.

That evening near the top of a hill not far from the village, we see them again. Mother and baby ride. The little donkey pulls his willing best. The father pulls at its side. The children push in silence at the back, legs aching. They glance at us, nod, and smile once more.

Azucena, which means 'lily' in English, is known as Zena; the villagers shorten all first names if they can, just as they use diminutives on every possible occasion, e.g. Carmen's daughter will be Carmenita or Ita, and our neighbours' precious son is Antonito.

Zena is not long widowed. Her husband, Pepe, in his declining years kept a small herd of goats. Zena has now only two, both nannies. She is short of money, she tells us as we meet her entering the market. Later we watch her from a discreet distance.

Dressed all in black, she stands patiently without moving, her bent back against the wheel of a cart. It is very hot, but the wall behind the cart casts its shadow over her, as she well knew it would.

She appears neither to see nor hear the kaleidoscope of animated people who bustle chattering in front of her; for them, market day is a day to be enjoyed to the full; no work, friends to see, and everything to buy, even if you don't buy anything.

The goat, udders almost reaching the ground and swollen with milk, presses closer against her knees.

Nobody while we watch comes to ask the price; nobody even glances at her. Madonna-shawl framing her humble face, she waits . . .

She comes to the market infrequently. All that we know about her is that she lives about ten kilometres from our village up the sparsely-peopled valley.

The big basket of chestnut-colour willow by her side is carefully covered from the scorching sun by a cloth which echoes the lapis lazuli of the arched sky.

We approach. She turns back a corner of the cloth, takes a bunch of sweet-smelling herbs from the basket, offers it to Joan.

'How much?'

She answers with grave dignity, 'One *duro*. With my herbs each meal will be a banquet.'

'I believe you.'

Joan smiles. Her returning smile is one of pure pleasure.

Joan buys the bunch and thanks her.

'*Gracias a usted, señora*,' she says. She holds out her hand. 'You have given me two *duros*. The price is one *duro*.'

Joan assures her there is no mistake – that big bunch for only five *pesetas*!

The woman reaches out and touches Joan's sleeve. We know this is to bring her good luck.

We smile at her as we walk away. 'I feel it has brought me

good luck too,' Joan says, and looks questioningly at me.
'I'm sure it has,' I say.

He is wiry, has abundant curls, is very swarthy; his almond eyes slope upward and away from his beaked thin nose.

Cigarettes behind his ears show startlingly white against his black hair. The cloth around his neck is dark red. Coat, trousers, sweater are very thick, boots hobnailed and sturdy. He is gesticulating as he talks. This *caminante*, this stranger passing through, is out to impress us in the bar. He uses his *mechero*, the wick hanging from the little tube, the toothed wheel as he thumbs it striking against the flint and providing the spark, to light a cigarette. He does not stop talking and gesticulating, now even more violently than before.

The young wife, barefoot at his side, has thin and dirty legs. The ragged skirt gapes across her pregnant belly. The child astride her hip tugs hard at her blouse, once brightly coloured. She does not look at him, but listens anxiously to her husband's rasping words.

The man turns to us, unashamedly begs money to give the child something to eat, a coffee for his wife. At once he turns his back on us, orders a brandy and coffee for himself. He moves away a step from the wretched girl, little more than a child herself, gulps the brandy and coffee, immediately demands another.

The girl gives the silent, wary child the bun, which it grasps tightly in both hands. Then, eyes closed, fingers surrounding the cup, she slowly, slowly sips . . .

We are glad to see him lead the way out. As soon as he is gone, the men decide that the money he spent was not obtained honestly, thus confirming their jaundiced view of all *gitanos*.

16

Life in the village is entirely family-centred. The villagers have friends, yes, as children have. But when you come to look into it, their permanent friends are always relatives, however distant. As they are never tired of telling you, the village is one great family – almost literally true because the majority are interrelated. What counts with them first and last is *la familia*. So it is that in the various *barrios*, grandfathers, sons and their families live next door to one another.

Age – 'to have many years', as they put it – is valued for itself, is given an honoured place in this society, is a matter for congratulation.

In my early days in the village, the old men would often ask me three questions, as if such questions were the common coin of everyday chat.

One, how old was I? They eyed me critically as they asked, hoping they were older. Showed their disappointment if they were not. Hastily mitigated it by pointing out I did not look my age because I had only worked with the pen, not the *asada*, which they pronounced *asah*, the big heavy tool-of-all work, spade, hoe and drill combined, the only tool apart from the machete they use.

Two, did I have a house in my country? Houses, real houses with more than one storey, gave prestige; *pisos*, flats, no.

Three, how much money did I have? When I said very little, they did not know whether to believe me or not. They were firmly convinced all foreigners must be rich compared to themselves. How else could they live in those splendid modern *chaletes*? Always *endomingados*, dressed in Sunday clothes? And with nothing at all to do . . . But this foreigner . . . Living among them . . . Never *endomingado* . . . Well, what he says *could* be the truth. If not, why else would he be working each day, writing in what he called the studio, to earn his bread? His *pan y cebolla*, bread and onions, as he always says to remind them of the days during and after the Civil War when they, *los viejos*, the old ones, had little or nothing else to eat.

Old folks are also, of course, so useful. When grandchildren first arrive, they often take them over and rear them. Very convenient for the working mothers; unbounded pleasure for the grandparents.

And as they grow older themselves, they still have an honoured place, are still acknowledged as head of the family; listened to, if not obeyed. When they are old enough to need help, they are fed, cleaned for and generally cosseted by their married daughters or daughters-in-law.

Many of the old people, as I have said, retain their exquisite natural manners and their natural piety.

One sign of this is their greeting, *Vaya usted con Dios*, Go with God. It is dying out among their children, though you can sometimes be pleasantly surprised to hear it in a young stranger's mouth.

We have been very moved from time to time by what Wordsworth called

> . . . that best portion of a good man's life,
> His little, nameless, unremembered acts
> Of kindness and of love.

Two little acts deserve mention.

When Pili owned the village store where we shop, I went to buy two kilos of sugar for the marmalade-making. Sugar then was in short supply: the Cuban beet sugar was exhausted, the local cane sugar not yet available.

Now Pili, as I've said, was a woman who believed herself a cut above the fellow villagers. She still retained her good looks, though by now somewhat faded. Hers was the biggest shop, with one of the biggest houses attached. And was not her husband the proprietor of a fine *cortijo* in the sierras with so much work to do? (So much, she could have added, he never came to the house in the village because, so the gossips darkly hinted, he had no need to.) As if this were not enough, she had a *muy intelligente* daughter who was training to be a schoolteacher, to be followed in due time by her two equally-clever sons.

Pili tartly told me she had no sugar to spare. All she had in stock was for her *clientes*, implying that I only came to shop when it suited me, preferring to spend my money elsewhere – which was true.

I happened to mention the incident when I later stopped to have a word with a group of old men sitting on a wall gossiping in the evening sun.

That same night, the old miller, Manolo Molinero, came to the door, a kilo of sugar under each arm. We were quite taken aback; we knew very well what it had cost him to walk all the way from his house to ours on his two bandy legs and arthritic knees – cripplingly arthritic.

He explained that Maria, *his* shopkeeper, had sold him the sugar for *lawingléh*, who were our guests and really needed it to make marmalade, which nobody in the village ever made or would ever contemplate making. How, they asked each other, could Pili, who prided herself on being a good Catholic, treat her neighbours so?

It took some time to persuade Manolo to accept payment, then to have a drink. Then, '*Échame la botella!*' he said, which means 'Throw the bottle at me', a phrase I have never forgotten. He chose the *rancio* rather than the Fundador: 'Brandy makes my poor old head go round like my waterwheel.'

We shook hands. I offered to walk him home; he scornfully refused. Filled with apprehension, we watched him tottering away. Hoped he would get home safely. We looked up at the preternaturally bright stars and blessed them for giving so much light this moonless night: Manolo could at least see where he was doing.

The only other time he came to see me was after I had tried to help him sell the huge mill for £3,000 to a millionaire who lived over the hill in a resplendent palace of a house – no chalet for him.

The deal fell through, and I was sorry; Manolo could have done with the money. But why was he here now talking about the deal?

At last I caught on. Even though there had been no sale, he had come to pay me the usual percentage of the price that intermediaries are given in such transactions. All the more astonishing when he must have been aware I knew nothing of such arrangements. But, of course, his honour was at stake among his neighbours; and he was a man of honour according to his own lights.

I burst out laughing. Assured him he owed me nothing. Would not have, even if there had been a sale; I was no businessman. Puzzled (relieved also, I'm sure), he shook his head – what a strange man this *ingléh* was. Finally he smiled, allowed me to *echar la botella* once again.

The other memorable little act of kindness shown to us was from Pepe, who with Manolo and others of their generation could be found on sunny evenings sitting chatting and smoking on their favourite wall.

When we first came to the village, we resolved we would never walk by anyone, known or unknown, man, woman or child, without at least passing the time of day. As often as possible, we enquired how they were, and took pains to address the older women as *señora*. And when we got to know them better, we would ask the women about their family, and the men about their crops and the prices, a topic of unfailing interest.

It was quite natural for us to treat everyone as equals, the habit of a lifetime, and we thought nothing of it. Imagine our amused surprise, then, to find that this became a seven-days wonder; behaviour so unexpected from foreigners as to be noted and gossiped about. As the old and highly respected ex-schoolmistress said to my neighbour, Isabel, knowing, perhaps, it would be brought straight back, '*Los ingleses*, your neighbours, they treat everybody alike, old and young, poor as well as rich. Who else here does that?'

Certainly we knew that Manolo and his fellows appreciated

our always stopping a moment to exchange a friendly word, especially when my grasp of the language increased sufficiently for us to crack a joke.

Early one evening Pepe, fat, unlined, smiling shyly, arrived at our door. Seated on the *terraza*, the only place to be on such lovely sunny evenings, he gladly accepted the brandy, wished us *salud*, health, drained his glass, and did not hesitate to hold it out for a refill.

Now relaxed, he handed Joan the small packet he had in his hand: '*Un regalito para usted, señora.*'

Joan cautiously opened the packet. The little gift inside turned out to be a doll-size pair of esparto sandals he had woven for her.

'How lovely,' Joan exclaimed. '*Muchísimas gracias.*'

'To remind you,' Pepe said, 'that we wore sandals like those during the Civil War and after. If our family did not pick the grass and make the sandals, then we had to go on bare feet.'

He needed no encouragement to launch into his account of the Civil War, so different from that of the Civil War Veteran.

We listened entranced, and were sorry when he said he must go. We sat for a while savouring the completely unexpected kindness he had shown us. And this from a man we had only from time to time had a word with . . . Something to be treasured . . .

In times of hardship, the families close ranks. Last year the prices the villagers were offered for their crops reached an all-time low: three *pesetas* for a kilo of tomatoes; six *pesetas* for a kilo of the finest peppers.

At this price they were not worth the carting. We were sad to see them thrown down in huge red and green heaps to rot in the sun.

No decent price was even offered to those farther up the valley for their first-quality table grapes, which were left to hang and shrivel on the vines, later to be gathered to make wine vinegar.

Some of our villagers were forced to borrow even more from the banks. All they were doing, they complained, was working for the banks, who were now charging them 17 per cent interest or more.

At the *matanzas*, only members of the extended family were invited. Each brought something to add to the junketing, or to be stored for future use. And instead of hiring *peones*, they helped each other out in the fields, working the necessary longer hours.

Even when the young people of marriageable age look outside the village to find their partner, it is often the son or daughter of someone who used to live in the village.

Further proof of this family-centredness you can see on the sun visor above the windscreens of their vans.

A very common statement reads, *Todo Por Mis Hijos*, Everything For My Children; another, *Todo Por Mis Nietos*, Everything For My Grandchildren.

The man with the largest family, except for the *gitano* already mentioned, proudly asserts on his sun visor, Everything For My Twelve Children. Two other fathers, each with 11 offspring, do the same thing.

When Padre Ramón asks them why they have so many, he always gets the same answer: 'It's the machine, Father, I must keep the machine working and in good order.'

Sometimes the father names his children: *Mi Marisol, Carmen Y Toni*; some display their wife's name: *Mi Rosario Y Yo*, My Rosario And I.

The widow Maria, she of the famed if minuscule black silk-and-lace pants, has one son, of whom she is inordinately proud. When he bought his first *furgoneta* (earth-shattering event), she demonstrated her overweening pride by insisting he had printed on his sun visor, Here Comes My Pepe, the clear implication being that all the world should stop and stare. Juan Sanchez and his wife have only one daughter. Following Maria's lead, he has on his sun visor, Follow My Gador And Aurora, to which challenge I always mentally add, If You Can, for she is the kind of *señorita* that would take some catching.

And to cap it all, the uncle of our young neighbour, Antonio, states, apparently without fear of contradiction, *Con Tres Basta*, With Three Enough.

The men faithfully attend five o'clock mass for their dead relatives, friends and acquaintances. They never enter the church, except for the mass for their parents, brothers and sisters. For everyone else, they stay huddled together outside, chattering, laughing, gesticulating, smoking – ah, those give-away-priced cigarettes.

Mass here is a happy occasion, social as well as religious. And why ever not if you believe that the dear departed are winging their way at that moment to *el paraíso*?

It is not surprising, then, that after family statements on the sun visors, the next most common are religious.

First come the appeals: May God Protect My Family And Me; May God Guide Us; May God Keep Us. Professions of faith are equally common: Secure In The Hands Of God; Nothing Without God: God Is Love – the name of Jesus being evoked as often as God's: Our Father Jesus; Jesus Above All; Jesus Our Salvation.

The most startling and thought-provoking I saw on a van parked outside Antonio's bar. It was not so much the juxtaposition of the names that startled me, but the order in which they were placed: El Greco And God.

El Greco, the Greek painter who settled in the sixteenth century in Toledo, that museum of a city that houses enough of his paintings to make a visit a most memorable experience, was one of the greatest religious artists that ever lived, that is beyond dispute. But to put him before God! A reminder, if reminder be needed, that you can never fathom how an Andalusian's mind works.

One Paco, the shortened form of Francisco, we call Franco because of his extreme right-wing views. Once a builder's labourer in the nearby town, he took up goats: 'I had no choice; the dust was choking me to death. I borrowed. Bought a small herd of goats. I was in luck. Almost every nanny had twins. The good billy I bought soon paid for itself. But I was not born to herd goats. Those hills! My poor knees and back! I was becoming an old man before my time. So I sold the herd and bought land. Now with my wife and son working with me, we are prospering – at last.'

'Is that why you've got those words on your sun visor?'

Paco laughed. 'Yes, because hard experience has taught me it is true.'

He then quoted with relish:

> *La Salud y pesetas*
> *Los demas son puñetas*
>
> Health and pence
> The rest is slaps in the face

Holy Cercio, as we call him, was one of only two men who used to attend mass regularly, but no longer. I like talking to him: his astonishing knowledge of the Bible reminds me of my grandfather, who believed every word in what he always referred to as the Good Book, a man who could give you chapter and verse for any quotation. On the sun visor of his old van, Cercio had these words: God Will Lead Us. His 'new' van had this desolating verse:

> *Bebi una y otra vez*
> *Pero nunca supe encontrar*
> *El agua para mi sed*
>
> I drank time and again
> But never knew how to find
> The water to quench my thirst

Some of the land in the *vega* belongs to men who do not live in the village, though probably their parents once did.

Two of their vans show quite clearly how far their owners have deserted long-established village ways. Each of their sun visors displays the name of a famous bullfighter. The first is Belmonte, the bandy-legged Sevillian revered as the type of the classic *torero*. The other is El Cordobés, the *gitano* who broke all the rules and by his sheer breathtaking courage revivified the modern *lidia*, bullfight.

Manuel, who lives at the end of Calle Cruces nearest the shop, has two sisters. The father was an alcoholic, fortunately now gone to join his forefathers.

Manuel's two sisters are the prettiest girls in the village – and that's saying something. When I described them to our neighbour Isabel as *guapa*, lovely, she firmly corrected me: '*Guapa*, no, Alberto. More than *guapa*, those girls are *hermosa*, beautiful.'

Manuel earns a scanty living carting vegetables and fruit from the *vega* plots to the wholesale cooperative which now handles what the villagers produce. His sisters have no dowry; neither, though coming up to 20, has a fiancé.

I wonder when I see Manuel's clapped-out old lorry as it rattles along how much longer it will hold out. Yet the one word blazoned in big letters I see on his sun visor I find as touching as any of the phrases quoted above.

The word is ROCINANTE. And Rocinante, you remember, was Don Quixote's spavined nag, the horse on which he charged the windmills and had so many incredible but immortal adventures.

How very quixotic of this likeable, earnest young man, shy and unworldly as he is, to call his ancient lorry after Don Quixote's steed. With two dowerless sisters, I fear he is going to need all his quixotism.

How pleased I was when in due course two discerning young townees came and carried away their *hermosas* prizes.

17

A most pleasing thing is that there is no age barrier here: old and young, including the very young, mingle as equals, take one another seriously.

The basis upon which this is built is that baby talk is unknown. From the beginning, parents talk to their children as they would to anyone else, expect them to behave as responsible human beings.

Girls as young as five or six become nanny to younger members of the family, totally responsible for them. An excellent job they make of it; and seem as eager to take on their young relatives when they have none in their own family.

The boys are just as eager to help their fathers and prefer working in the fields to going to school. Many, in fact, see little of the village classroom. The only education they need they will get by their father's side, an opinion their fathers usually share. Many children are consequently under no more pressure to attend than are the gypsy children, who never go to school. And mothers with large families are no keener to see that their little nursemaids go.

Many of the boys grow up with only the scantiest grasp of reading and writing, or none at all. Yet, like their fathers, they can all calculate, do sums in their head that would baffle me. In this macho society, fathers in particular pray for a son.

Children of all ages in our *barrio* often give us proof of this lack of age barrier. If either of us happen to be coming home at the same time as a child, he or she will wait or hurry to catch us up so that we can make our way chatting together.

I remember one incident in particular. A little girl with raven-black curls would always link hands with Joan whenever possible. From the *terraza* I would see them coming, Joan slowly – this was in our earliest days – enunciating her English, the child her dialect, both happy and at ease.

It is a strange combination, this spoiling them to death on the one hand, this treating them as adults capable of accepting responsibility, of doing useful jobs, on the other. But it works. You have only to watch children at the *matanzas*, see them gladly busy about the little tasks they have been given, settle to eat, then go to play while their elders relax.

The children do not change their attitude as they become teenagers. The boys, of course, become a little more sedate, a little more conscious of their sex as they talk to Joan. The girls do not change at all, remain as outgoing and relaxed as before, with seemingly no consciousness whatsoever of their sex when talking to me. They accept my compliments as they have always accepted them – with sincere pleasure.

What makes this possible is that they feel so secure: first, in their Catholic faith; second, because they see themselves members of one great family; and therefore not at risk from any man.

As for the toddlers of both sexes, they wander freely about the village, go in and out of the houses, welcomed everywhere, talked to by everyone – such a joy.

The mothers have no trouble in summoning them home. They simply stand in their doorways or on their *terraza* and shout: 'Pakeeee . . . to! Carmeneeee . . . ta!' Sound travels well here, and they know they will be heard all over the village.

Crops like runner beans are supported by *cañaveras*, the ditch reeds which fortunately grow in such abundance here, often to a height of 20 feet or more.

Each man has his own essential supply, growing around his plots, along the nearby river banks, or anywhere on wet ground. Not often does a man buy canes; but it has been known, for he cannot do without them.

They cut and trim the canes with the machete and fire the area soon after – necessary to ensure that a new crop, supple and strong, will grow. Old canes are useless, breaking easily under the weight of the crop, totally unable to give in the wind.

Tomatoes are heavier and need to have a supporting framework of poles, bought and used year after year until no longer fit to do the job.

An immense amount of work is needed to make these supports. Each hole for each *caña* is made by a long crowbar lifted and driven into the soil by sheer muscle power. There is considerable work, also, in clearing the supports, cutting the ties from the haulms, harvesting the haulms as mule and goat fodder and bedding, bundling the poles and those *cañas* good enough to use another time ... Work enough, when you remember they take three crops a year from this fertile land.

This *vega* has been cultivated for at least 3,000 years. The Phoenicians established a trading post where the village now stands, others being established at Cádiz, Málaga and Almuñecar.

Their domination lasted from 11,000 BC until 680 BC, when the Greeks took over. Another hundred years and they were replaced by the Syrians from Carthage. Two centuries on, and they were ousted by what the Andalusians insist on calling the Moors, i.e. Mussulmen from the north coast of Africa. And they in their turn, as we have seen, were driven out by the Catholic monarchs, Ferdinand and Isabella, at the end of the fifteenth century.

It is a tribute to the villagers and their forefathers that the fertility of this soil has been maintained. Heavy dunging at least once a year is the basis. In recent times, this has been supplemented by nitrate from Chile. Regular and careful spraying, especially against potato blight, is essential – against insect damage, too.

Only once have we seen the whole of an early crop of potatoes, to be lifted in March, totally ruined by a severe blight. The young owner of this large oblong plot over the river suffered such opprobrium that he learnt his lesson once for all: never again would he attempt to cut corners and costs.

Our *agricultores* by and large stick to the tried and traditional

147

crops – potatoes, tomatoes, lettuce, kidney beans, courgettes, aubergines, watermelons. On the sides of their plots you will from time to time see cabbage, cauliflower, carrots, onions growing, but these are only for the house.

Peas are the main crop farther inland in sheltered dry valleys, such as that below Albuñol; the sight of the mangetout's purple flowers always makes our mouth water. Peas do not, however, do well enough in our valley to make it worthwhile growing them.

Habas, broad beans, were until recently an important crop here. No longer: they now suffer from a mysterious disease that turns the haulms yellow and stunts the beans. What is it? No one I ask has any real idea; the only thing they come up with is that the land is sick of the beans. But why? They only shake their head.

Sometimes the more adventurous of our young *agricultores* try a new crop. One of our neighbours sowed sweetcorn and excitedly told us what a good price he would get. The whole crop failed.

Over the last three seasons some have tried a new cos lettuce because it brings in more money than their traditional and trusted variety. The great heaps of mouldering lettuce by the side of their plots or cast into the dry river bed testify to the utter disaster the experiment proved.

One of Juan José's many plots lies near our *casa* in a very sheltered spot. Here Juan José began to grow peas and mangetout successfully.

As soon as they came into flower our mouths began to water: we could almost taste the mangetout as we contemplated their lovely colours from out *terraza*.

I urged Joan to allow me to go and see if I could buy some; Juan was not somebody we expected to offer us any after our contretemps over his clever daughter, Evedina. Joan reluctantly agreed, but refused to come herself for fear of a rebuff.

I called on Juan. After the customary glass of wine – Juan never drank spirits, they made his head also turn like a windmill

– I asked if I could buy some peas from time to time as they became ready.

My question was greeted with what appeared to be genuine horror. *Buy?* Certainly not! *Cielos*, heavens, were we not *buenos vecinos*, good neighbours? And did not neighbours here in our village give each other what the other lacked? Always have, and always will.

Juan José put his hand on my shoulder. 'So, Alberto *hombre*, help yourself. That *parcela* is yours and Juanita's. Take what you want, when you want . . . After all, it will be very little. You are only two. You have no hungry mouths to feed. And, as your neighbours tell me, you eat very little.'

He waved away my sincere thanks. Well pleased (what a good tale to tell his neighbours), he escorted me to the door. There his wife was waiting to give me a big bag of tomatoes, peppers and lettuce – for Juanita!

We did indeed take advantage of his incredibly kind offer, he being what he was. I tried to conceal my slight sense of triumph at my coup; Joan spotted it and said she was pleased I could still act as I used to (according to her) when I thought I had scored a little victory. We selected only the tenderest of both kinds of peas. What a contrast they were to the field peas we were able to buy in the market.

From then on, peas, especially mangetout, became a regular feature of Joan's cuisine.

This field of peas, hemmed in by dry hills, promised too little and was abandoned.

A ragged *gitano*, wife and five children, keep close together, as if what they do is illicit. Their wide sombreros banish the blazing sun and shut in their absorbed silence.

They stretch forward, search every haulm scrupulously, strip off the pods, push them into the big sacks they drag. They move, earth-colour and urgent, among the yellowing stalks.

Suddenly they see that we are standing above them on the hillside. They straighten and are still as we are watching.

We exchange no word or gesture. They stand, anxious until

149

they are sure we offer no threat, then bend with new urgency to harvest what has been allowed to rot.

After a crop has been cleared from the *vega* below us, we wait with as much interest as we have always had for the ploughing to begin.

The plough is still the simple one which their forefathers used, fastened to a rough-hewn sapling trunk which goes between the pair of mules and secured to their hames.

Ploughing with a pair of mules pulling this rudimentary plough is a skilful and taxing job; by the end of the day both man and sweat-lathered mules are tired out.

The furrows are not straight; they follow the shape of the plot. At the end of each furrow, the man lifts and drags the heavy plough around; the mules stand patiently, glad of the second's rest, only moving when their master shouts '*Mooool*,' or one of his incomprehensible command words.

Only rarely does the plougher carry a stick, and only then a slender *caña* to flick the mules with occasionally, his shouts and shaken reins usually sufficient encouragement.

Ploughing here in the *vega* on the level is hard work enough. Imagine, then, what labour it must be on the steeply sloping side of an Alpujarran mountain. Little wonder we have often stopped to gaze incredulously at some little scarecrow of a man and his two intrepid mules gallantly working their serpentine way along some impossible slope among the olives or vines, waiting apprehensively for man, mules and plough to come crashing down.

The Alpujarras! So beautiful, so wild, so totally unspoiled!

Another most welcome feature, we discovered in our first year, was that Christmas had not yet been degraded by creeping commercialisation: no pseudo joy, no manufactured jollity, no false bonhomie, no gluttonous gorging, no buy, buy, buy. What a refreshing contrast to what has long been the standard in our Christian [*sic*] country.

As non-believers, we had abandoned this farrago after our

three daughters left home, although eternally grateful before that for the lovely make-believe: the shining tree with the Christmas fairy and her silver chain that had been in the family for generations, Santa Claus and the nocturnal-filled stockings, the loving giving and receiving of gifts. Eternally regretful, also, we could not answer Betjeman's question in the affirmative:

> And is it true? And is it true,
> This most tremendous tale of all,
> Seen in a stained-glass window's hue,
> A Baby in an ox's stall
> The Maker of the stars and sea
> Become a Child on earth for me?

Here in the village Christmas Day is like any other day. The men go to work in the fields, the women busy themselves about their daily tasks, the children holiday as usual. No tree, no presents, no Christmas dinner.

The event that sets this day apart is the midnight mass. This, surely, is as it should be for what is, after all, a religious festival. And then the children band together, as I've said, and come around the village, blowing horns and whistles, beating drums, banging anything they can lay their hands on, to celebrate the birth of the Child: *El Señor*.

Absolute bedlam, reminding me – how inappropriately – of *la cencerra* which drove Gafas's widow and her retarded lover apart.

18

Padre Ramón was our new village *cura*. Young, impetuous, energetic, he decided at once to do something about the cemetery.

'These villagers have been discussing it for years,' he said. 'Nothing has been done. *Mañana*, always *mañana*. I have already found that here in Andalusia there is never any tomorrow ... We Northerners are, *gracias a Dios*, different.' He paused and looked at me, his eyes shining with mischief behind his huge horn-rims. 'We Northerners –'

'You're from Burgos, I believe, where they speak perfect Castilian.'

Padre Ramón did not miss the irony in my voice. He smiled and shrugged. 'We do, yes, or so we think. But if the truth be told, those of Valladolid speak the classical Castilian.' He smiled again, a thing some of the villagers already were puzzled by. 'The difficulty here is that I am only now getting to understand what my parishioners say to me. Their dialect –'

'You don't need to tell me, Father. They swallow all the consonants and –'

'Exactly. Their grammar, also, or rather their lack of it.'

We smiled at each other wryly, the familiar look of fellow sufferers.

The village cemetery was shared by another village, El Chico, farther up the river. The top row of the four rows of *nichos*, niches, that backed onto the church wall belonged to the El Chico people. No one had visited the *nichos* for many a long year. The rents had not been renewed; the roofs were falling in. It was clear to Ramón that the families owning the *nichos* had died out, or that they were no longer living in El Chico. Little wonder,

152

Ramón thought, the village was so isolated – no church, no indoor sanitation, no decent road, no bar; such villages were slowly dying everywhere in this impoverished province.

Space in our cemetery was getting scarcer every year. It was indeed high time the *nichos* were cleared out, repaired, and sold to new customers.

As I've said, doña Antonia and doña Pasión are the two ladies who organise *everything* in the church. They knew Padre Ramón wished the work to begin at once, but he would need a little ready cash to pay Manolo Nicho to do the work. Accordingly, they went around the village with the hat; we, of course, were included, much to our satisfaction.

Father Ramón himself supervised the work: he already knew, apparently, that Manolo was more fond of smoking and gossiping on the job than working.

I went down to the cemetery to see how the work was getting on. What surprised me about the remains as Manolo scraped them out from the niches was the colour – not white, as I expected, but a rusty orange.

It had always struck me as odd that the top row of niches should be cheapest, at present about £50 a niche. Now was the time to find out why.

I kept a perfectly straight face as I said, 'It seems to me, Father, that the top row should be dearest, not cheapest. After all, they are nearer heaven than the others. The people in them will have a head start when the great day comes. As for us, we intend to buy one of the top ones. Juanita, my wife, tells me that she will sit up and see what I'm doing on the *terazza* – if she goes first, that is.'

'I know nothing about the way you English think,' the *cura* said in mock seriousness. 'But I do know about the character of these villagers – Fausto has already taught me. No, these villagers are not thinking of heaven, that you must understand. No, certainly not. All they are thinking of is their prestige. This is the reason the second and third rows are always sold first. They are the dearest.'

My face showed my genuine puzzlement.

Father Ramón grinned. 'It is the mentality of these Southerners.

153

They buy the second and third rows instead of the top and bottom precisely because they are the dearest . . .'

I shook my head, more puzzled than ever.

'You must remember that a *nicho* is sold to a family long before it is needed. Everyone in the village knows which *nicho* has been bought by which family. A family would lose face if it did not buy one of the dearest. So all except the very poor do.'

'Well, well.'

'You must also take into account the visitors from the town and other villages – relatives mostly, everybody in the district seems to be related in some way or other. Perhaps this . . .'

There was no need for Ramón to finish his statement; was I not also a foreigner like himself in this community?

'When relatives and friends come to a funeral,' he continued, 'they all go into the cemetery after the mass to witness the coffin being sealed in its *nicho*. Afterwards, they stay to read the names on the occupied *nichos*, and to study the photographs, but only those of the second and third rows.'

'Why only those?'

'They can read those without looking up or stooping down. '

'Ah, I see. Too much bother.'

'No, not at all. It's simply that they would not wish to be seen to be so curious. '

Manolo, because he was being closely supervised, soon cleared all the El Chico niches. Little remained in each except what appeared to be orange dust and the similar-coloured remains of bones.

Ramón carefully put the contents of each niche into its own little hessian bag. He tied their necks and attached to each bag a label with the details of the family concerned. He carried the bags around to the back of the church and stacked them in a corner against the church wall.

In his haste to get the job done, Ramón had omitted to visit El Chico to check whether anyone there still had an interest in a niche. Yet there was no need, of that he was sure. Had not those two pearls of women, doña Antonia and doña Pasión assured him no families with any claim to the *nichos* were left?

154

Despite this, he had taken the precaution of sacking the remains. We knew why: the bones of one's ancestors were revered above all else here. When the *pantano*, the huge reservoir high in the Alpujarras, was being built, destined to relieve Almería of its perpetual problem of water shortage, we visited the little village before it was drowned. After it was flooded, we went to see its cemetery high up on a nearby hill. It was as we had previously seen it in the village: the niches rebuilt, each containing its remains and the family details in place on the niche fronts.

Rainstorms rarely happen in our village. When they do occur, the rain sheets down as if trying to make up for the months of drought. One such rainstorm happened while the bones were lying against the church wall.

It was old Father Fausto who pointed out once again that Ramón really ought to go to El Chico to tell them the *nichos* has been cleared – just in case ... Felix told Ramón that was his opinion also: the three priests were still living together (there are always three).

Ramón, in deference to Fausto's age, if not to his judgement, and out of respect for Felix, set off up the narrow, winding path, sufficiently steep to make him stop from time to time to get his breath, without checking the bags.

Imagine his and everyone else's surprise when the very next week two *matrimonios*, married couples, arrived to claim their ancestors' bones.

Ramón gladly led them around to the back of the church. He bent down to sort out the two bags from the others. He could not – the storm had completely washed the ink from the labels.

The older man and his wife were very understanding. 'It is an act of God, Father. What can we do about it? Nothing. The bones – *¡qué descansen en paz!* – can go with the others into the ossuary.'

The other couple seemed to take leave of their senses. They burst into tears, howling like demented dogs. As soon as the gross wife saw the women from the nearby houses beginning to congregate, she found her tongue.

'What right have you, a priest appointed by God, to move the

155

sacred bones from their *nichos* without permission? Why did you not send for us? Why, once removed from their resting place, did you leave the sacred bones *outside* the church? At least they should have been put *inside* God's own holy house.'

By now men were joining the women. How right they had been, they congratulated themselves. In their opinion, this young priest – this Northerner – had a lot to learn. Why, when Father Fausto was their parish priest, he consulted everybody before he did anything new. It had taken him years to fathom their ways, but fathom them he had.

The husband, a leathery-faced, bulbous-nosed man over six feet, noted the presence of the men. A triumphant look spread over his lined face. It was time now he showed everybody what an aggrieved and faithful son and grandson felt about this wilful desecration.

He stepped forward, putting himself between Ramón and his wife. He turned. 'Shut up, woman!' he shouted, pushing her violently backwards.

Ramón, thinking it was all over and thanking *El Señor*, opened his mouth to say how sorry he was. It was useless: the man was now shouting louder than his wife had done.

'Do you realise that my ancestors' bones are in that sack? All of them? I love my father, my grandfather, my mother, my grandmother – *¡qué descansen en paz!* – more than anything else on earth. You have robbed me of my dearest wish. My dearest wish is to be buried with the bones of my ancestors. Now what is going to happen? What are you, a priest appointed by God, going to do about it?'

Ramón had no useful suggestion to make. Even if he had, the man was in no mood to listen; never had he had such an audience hanging on his every word. To be able to abuse a priest. And quite rightly, too. To win the argument. Just think of the story he would tell when he got back to El Chico. He stood there, waving his arms wildly, repeating himself over and over again.

There were by now more curious and delighted onlookers than ever. Ramón decided that enough was enough. He turned tail, rushed out of the cemetery, jumped into his blue *Deux Chevaux* and headed with all possible speed for home.

156

It was Fausto who, in his perfect wisdom, thought of the solution. I asked him to tell me about it.

'Well, Alberto, I saw that all the bones – what was left of them, that is – in all the bags would only fill one big bag, leaving out the dust, for what use is dust? Most of the bones had just powdered away. This dry climate, you see, after all this time.'

I nodded. 'And so?'

'I asked doña Antonia and doña Pasión to make me a beautiful white linen bag, big enough to hold all the remains of bones.'

'To put *all* the bones in, and . . .'

'Exactly. On the bag they embroidered a fine cross. Below it they put the details of the man's family: full names, dates of birth and death.'

I shook my head in admiration of such inspired ingenuity. 'And did that satisfy the couple?'

'Completely. They were most grateful to Father Ramón. The husband was going to keep the bag on a little table below the Virgin Mary on the mantelpiece. When his time came, he would have the bag buried with him. Then his dearest wish would be fulfilled.'

Father Fausto paused, and I savoured once again the delightful Victorian English he spoke so fluently with a Welsh accent.

'You see, Alberto, who am I to judge? As the man said, now there could be no possible mistake. He was now utterly sure he was going to be buried with his ancestors' bones.'

He sighed, seemingly somewhat sad. Then, with a twinkle in his eye and a smile on his lips, he added: 'Being a Northerner from Burgos, as are Fathers Felix and Ramón, I'm afraid I shall never understand these superstitious Southerners.'

19

You can't buy a dream; but you *can* buy sunshine at too dear a price.

The Macclesfields (that's where they came from) arrived on our doorstep one sunny winter's day. They were, it transpired, of the ilk that believed they would be welcome; after all, they were English, they'd heard we were also, and therefore . . .

'Tea?' I asked hopefully when Joan had settled them on the *terraza*.

The quick look they exchanged of surprise, if not of actual dismay, was answer enough.

'We've beer, wine, and —'

I hastily interrupted Joan. I had no DYC, that abominable substitute for whisky so many expats drink, and I certainly wasn't going to offer these intruders my good whisky.

'Beer, white or red wine,' I said.

They made their choice, and sat eating Joan's *tapas* of good mountain ham on fresh bread. Why, I asked myself, had she not given them something else — *jamon serrano* costs an eye — but that was Joan.

The man turned out to be a veritable Balaam's ass, making punk jokes, then immediately braying deafeningly. The woman proved almost from the first word what in my Cornish childhood we called a 'Crying Grace'. However, as we listened to their story, which they were eager to unfold, we admitted to ourselves she had much to cry about.

They had emigrated three years ago. Bought a small apartment in Roquetas de Mar, a pleasant enough resort, if you like that sort of thing. Their cash was in short supply, and they lived carefully, if not to say meagrely. They had not reckoned on the steadily-rising prices, so they cut their cloth accordingly.

So far, so good. The husband, tempted by a salesman, sold the apartment and bought a chalet – ah, that magic word! – in a German-owned and run *conurbación*, new settlement, some distance to the east of Roquetas and on a hill with an uninterrupted view of the sea.

They had seen the chalet before they bought it. Approved of it, of the German-clean roads and tidy gardens, but had omitted to find out exactly what the outgoings were, or to ascertain they would rise each six months. Consequently, they were now in dire straits.

The wife then took up the story. Her first beef was that they were now having to dip into their very limited capital to keep afloat, so where would it all end? Her second was that they found that they could not sit out of doors for many months of the year; in winter because the wind blew so hard; in summer because of the cursed flies. And, to cap it all, the Germans in residence had made it clear they wanted nothing to do with them.

'Rich snobs, that's what they are,' she whined. 'They won't even speak English to us, though we know they can.'

The pair came unbidden once a week for the next five weeks. Joan received them in her usual hospitable and kindly way, while I became increasingly cold and irritated. At each visit, they invited us to go and see the chalet. We didn't; I had to insist on this; Joan out of the kindness of her heart would have gone.

At the end of the five weeks, they got the message and came no more . . .

An admirable engineer and his devoted wife live over the hill from us. The *parcela* on which they built their chalet was one of 60 or so jointly owned by a rich Englishman and an equally rich German; it was cheap, a real bargain.

We became firm friends with the Scot and his lively, indomitable wife. They were one of the first to buy into what the owners assured them would develop into a thriving settlement: it never did. No post, no baker, no fishman, no *butano*, calor gas, delivery then, ten years ago, or now. All right, if you have nothing better to do than go traipsing daily into the nearest town, but . . .

Because they were one of the first to buy, and at such a very, very reasonable price, they had the ideal position, nothing between them and the Med in the far distance but scrub frequented only by goatherds. They believed they had indeed bought their dream.

Angus, the husband, had worked the previous ten years in Israel – in munitions, he shamefacedly confessed some time after we got to know them, his wife doing a part-time job as library assistant. They had lived in a stiflingly small flat in Tel Aviv, saving and scaping to retire early to their dream home on the Costa de Almería; their view of the Israelies is unprintable.

They had reckoned without the local climate: daily sunshine, yes; but high humidity, savage winds blowing over this exposed hillside, and the accompanying dust, sometimes the red Saharan dust that clung to the impeccable white façade of their chalet (they were extremely house-proud), which Angus at once repainted.

Two years ago, the locals brought water from a newly discovered well near us up to the useless scrub in front of our friends' chalet. In a short while, the scrub became transformed into *invernaderos*, plastic houses. You can well imagine what this meant: the noise, the dust, their peace shattered.

Their dream shattered as well. They have no possibility of escape. Nobody will buy the chalet now, even though Angus, as skilled in wood as in metal, had turned house and garden into something that would grace the pages of any of the glossy magazines devoted to such things . . .

We met the man in a bar in Almuñecar, the centre of the avocado-growing region. We judged him in his early fifties, although he looked much older; white-haired, lean-faced, thin, harassed-looking.

He was eager to tell his story. He had realised his dream and bought an avocado orchard for a very cheap price: the Spaniard had become ill, wanted to get out, and so . . .

The trees, the Spaniard averred, would begin to bear the next

160

year; it was a great advantage to have young and vigorous trees.

That was five years ago. No fruit for the first three years. The new owner was patient. The reason, he then discovered, was that all his trees were female – and you have to have males to fertilise them. Only now is he beginning to get the rudiments of a crop; but he doubts whether he will ever become successful. As for his dream . . .

Dreams. We were reminded of a pair living on a precipitous hillside up a narrow, steep, twisting track about 15 kilometres from us. They had bought the little peasant house because you could on a clear day see Africa. No sewage, no water indoors, no electricity, but the house was so cheap that it was a gift, or so they thought. When they went into the cost of installing these amenities, they were shocked at the price. The last time we saw them coming down their track, they told us they were still camping out in the house, and that, *poco a poco*, little by little, they would add the amenities.

In some ways, the saddest case of the many we could relate, was the old man we met at Roscoff waiting for the boat. An experienced pig farmer, he and his wife had bought a pig farm in Andalusia because they both suffered from arthritis and had been told the sun was their saviour. Besides, they had always dreamed of living in Spain.

The first five years, all had gone well. They had made a living, all that they wanted, and the sun had helped considerably to relieve their pain.

Last year the government had removed the price control on feedstuffs, but had kept it on the price of pork: end of the possibility of making a fair living.

He showed us the huge bag of walnuts he was taking to England to sell. This should help, if only for a while; his wife would be waiting to hear how much he'd got.

Our van was next to his ancient Morris shooting brake. We had to turn away as we saw the Customs men confiscating his precious sack . . .

As for falling ill if you live in our region, don't, especially if you have only bothered to acquire shopping Spanish.

The nearest hospital to us – you'll be lucky if they give you a drink of water. No, it's your own kin that must attend and feed you.

As for communicating, your shopping Spanish will get you nowhere. And an interpreter? Why should they bother with such a person? This foreigner has probably been living here since Franco's time. Welcome then, because he had hard currency, and given all sorts of privileges. But now, Spain was a democracy – and a democracy treats all alike.

To hear these foreigners grumble. Those in Denia, *por ejemplo*, who had many years ago built their *chaletes* illegally too near the shore. Now the government had caught up with them. Drawn the line the land side of their *chaletes*. Told them – this is a democracy – they can live in the *chaletes* until they die; then the property becomes the property of the government.

As for their constant grumbles about the new taxes, they must now pay the same as everyone else: in a democracy, all must share the burden.

20

The *ayuntamiento*, the council, in the nearest town is legally responsible for our village.

One of the villagers' perpetual complaints is this: they pay the same rates and taxes as the townsfolk, but they get little or no benefit, even though they have their own *alcalde*, mayor, who has the right of attending all the council meetings, which he rarely does, having given up hope long ago.

Fifteen years ago, the wide but very rutted and potholed dusty track that connected village and town, an absolute headache to drive – you had to proceed like a sidewinder – was made into a decent road with a smooth if thin tarmac surface.

The villagers couldn't believe their luck. At last the *ayuntamiento* had granted what they had been petitioning for 20 years. What a pleasure it was to go to town on mule back, on a donkey, or walking, if you had to.

The very next year, a flash flood high up in the Sierra Nevada thundered down the valley, washing away tracks and houses and cultivated land, and drowning people and animals in its path. The whole valley was declared a disaster area; compensation was paid to those who had lost houses, land and animals (chiefly goats, mules and donkeys).

Over the next few years, the houses were rebuilt, the land and tracks restored, all except our village road. The flood had completely destroyed it: no vestige of tarmac remained, and it was now worse than ever.

The town council turned a deaf ear to the villagers' pleas. There was no more money. It had all been spent on the road last year. Was such an act of God their fault? Of course not. What would be, would be. It was *sin remedio*, without remedy.

An act of God, yes. The villagers accepted it with that typical Andalusian shrug, head to one side, hands lifted, palm up.

Last year, the roadmen and their machines arrived out of the blue. The road was once again tarmacked. What a joy now to go to town, especially in the *furgoneta* if they had one, that noisy, uncomfortable tin box of a workhorse, on market days and fiestas.

The town council had been astonishingly generous. Enough money was left over to make a new village main street, right up to a few metres from our house in Calle Cruces, where the money ran out. The old people in particular were pleased; it was so much easier to go to and fro to the shops, and to take the air occasionally.

That was last year. This year, again without warning, the specialist gang arrived to lay sewage pipes where none existed, and to replace the old one in the main street.

A young man from Granada was in charge of the big mechanical digger. It began at the entrance to the village and dug a trench, three metres deep, one metre wide, right up through the main street, completely destroying the tarmac and throwing the rubble against the sides and front doors of the houses.

The main street dramatically narrows as it goes up through the village. This is where the real problem began. The mechanical digger was a truly heroic machine. Its long digging and grappling arm made nothing of driving down through the shaley rock on which the houses were built. And its sheer power was matched by the almost human flexibility and range of movements of its arm.

It was an English machine, a Hy-Mac Whitlock. I felt rather proud when this was pointed out to me every time I passed the driver. But it had two grave weaknesses. The first was that it was just too big to work where the main street narrowed. Yet work it did, gouging out great pieces from the cob walls and tearing down their drainpipes from the guttering above.

Its second weakness was that, in digging the trench, it grubbed up and shattered everything in its path. When I tell you this included the water pipes and the old sewer itself, you can visualise the scene and the reactions of the householders: fountains and stench everywhere.

164

According to them, the original sewer had only been laid a few years ago and was perfectly satisfactory. Why, then, lay this enormous sewer in the middle of the street, so much deeper than the old? Their complaints, loud and vehement and sustained, were targeted on the boss of the gang.

He was a harassed-looking man with prematurely grey hair and moustache. With what patience he could muster, he explained that the trouble was where the sewage went – through open channels after leaving the sewer, and so to the sea. This was a danger to themselves and to others, no longer acceptable in modern democratic Spain.

Well, even if that were so, which they all doubted, why couldn't the work have been done before the tarmac was laid down last year?

The boss could only reply that they would have to ask the *ayuntamiento*, it was no affair of his.

'I will tell you why,' said Francisco, an old man who had fought on Franco's side at the Battle of the Ebro. 'We have no democracy here. We are in the hands of the bureaucracy – and the bureaucracy is a *burro*!'

This was rich, I thought, coming from one who was a Falangist, the wielders of the most rigid bureaucracy Spain has ever known.

Although the water was turned on occasionally at night, we could only rely on it on Sundays. Fortunately, repairing the broken sewage pipe was given priority, so the householders had only to suffer for a day or two.

The village women complained most bitterly at the lack of water: how could they be expected to keep their family's clothes clean if there was no water in the *pila*, the big cement washtub outside at the back of their house?

Even the young women who had deserted the old ways and got their drinking and cooking water from the tap, now had to fetch it from La Patrona, a chore they bitterly resented.

In the side streets – paths, rather – the gang had to use mechanical drills. The din from these, and from Hy-Mac itself, from eight in the morning till eight at night, was very hard to put up with, and we all prayed for a speedy end.

165

One thing puzzled me. The enormous new sewer was being laid expertly by the side of the old sewer; this I could see. But each section was being covered in as it was laid. But what about the connections from the houses to the sewer? The old sewer, so carefully repaired, was obviously still doing its duty.

I buttonholed the boss just before he went off to lunch one day. The connections? They were no part of his contract. His job was to lay the new sewer, and to put right any accidental damage, that was all.

And what about the surface of the street, now a mass of uneven rubble? That was up to the people who lived in the street, that was what was done in other villages. And the connections? They were the responsibility of the *ayuntamiento*. When would the houses be connected?

He shrugged. 'There isn't any more money. This year, next year, *depende . . .*' Then he smiled. 'But I can tell you one thing for sure. They'll all have to pay.'

'Who will?' I asked, more puzzled than ever.

'The people here in the village. Each house will have to pay to be connected . . . Pay dearly.'

'How much?'

'At least 25,000 *pesetas*.'

This was about £75, a fortune to the villagers. Why on earth was it so high?

'*Hombre*, the council must get their money back. They can't go bankrupt.'

'But the new sewer doesn't reach some houses – mine, for instance. So we can't be connected, can we?'

'The money ran out. No matter, you'll all have to pay as well as the others.'

'Surely not!'

'Of course, yes. That's what happened in every village we've done. In a democracy, it's only right that all share the burden, each man helping his neighbour. Don't you agree?'

I checked this with the Hy-Mac driver, whom I had named *El creador de surtidores*, the creator of fountains, a title he seemed inordinately proud of.

'True,' he said. 'We're all living in a democracy now, *amigo*.'

He winked and smiled broadly. 'We're modelling ourselves on you English. That'll please you, I'm sure.'

One night, I went out for a breath of air. A figure was crouched in the darkness over the huge manhole cover a few metres from our door which marked the end of the new sewer.

By now, my eyes being used to the darkness, I recognised him. It was Juan White Mule, my near neighbour.

'Hola, Juan, que pasa?'

'Todo finito, Alberto.'

'What's just finished, Juan?'

He looked at me as if I were a bit *memo*, soft in the head, to ask.

'You remember, Alberto, the leak in my old sewer pipe? And you saw me replacing it with a new one?'

'Yes.'

'Well, it's still not satisfactory, the pipe must be clogged farther down towards the *acequia*, the irrigation channel.'

'So?'

'So I've connected my new pipe to the new sewer. Help me to put back the manhole cover.'

I did as he asked.

He laughed, as well he might. 'Now, Alberto, I shall not have to pay to be connected, will I?'

I had always admired Juan's shrewdness. Now my admiration knew no bounds.

21

After we had been living in the village for a decade or so, we came back from a fortnight's break in Portugal to find our house had been burgled. The entry had been made through a narrow pane in one of the french windows that opened onto the *terraza*.

Joan was upset to see everything strewn over the floor. Yet, as I was quick to point out, there was no wilful damage, nor any parting gift of urine and faeces.

How lucky we were, we soon concluded. The only thing missing was a little screwdriver. We suspected one of the *gitano* children, perhaps one from the families that were constantly coming and going in the gypsy *barrio*, for he and his dog had slept on one of our beds.

Two years later, someone got in through the door at the back of our bedroom, the door that gives access to our little hillside 'garden' – doubtless after non-existent money and jewellery, as was the boy.

By now we were quite philosophical: tidying up was a little price to pay for being privileged to live in what was for us an enchanted haven.

My aplomb was shattered when I discovered that my big manual typewriter, which had served me so well here, was the only thing missing.

It was Joan who now pointed out to me with a certain relish that there was no wilful damage, so how lucky we were, etc.

No longer were we living in days when we could all leave our doors unlocked, our houses unattended, as had always been our neighbours' proud boast: nothing was ever stolen in *our* village, nothing.

My neighbours blamed the recently arrived *gitano* who with his numerous brood was now squatting in the empty house at the end of Calle Cruces. A stranger, but of course related to the *gitanos* in the *barrio gitano*: were they not all of one tribe?

We know this *gitano* well by sight. A little ferrety man, his white hair startling above his dark face, he carried as his constant companion a ghetto blaster turned on at full volume as he passed to and fro in front of our door.

I buttonholed him soon after this nuisance began. He was genuinely astonished that I objected to the din. Was it not music? Did not everyone here love music? What, then, was my objection?

I firmly told him. He was disturbing our peace. In particular, my wife found the noise distressing – bringing your wife in is always a telling point here. He nodded his understanding. We foreigners were different. Yet he knew we were good friends with everybody, he would be a good friend also.

He still carried his ghetto blaster with him. Now he turned it off when he judged he was near enough for us to hear it, and turned it on again when he judged he was at a safe distance away.

At least twice a week he was escorted – half carried, rather – from the bar by a jovial pot-bellied gypsy who smiled conspiratorially at us as he passed. As the squatter was utterly unable to walk unaided, we named him Legless.

We did not believe this little man was the culprit. We were sure he was harmless: who among us hasn't their little weaknesses? But where, especially with so many mouths to feed, did he get the money to get drunk?

We soon found out. Often, on our shopping visits to town, Legless would be squatting at the entrance to a supermarket, his begging tin extended, and smoking, a thing I, in my intolerance, found it hard to take when a beggar was begging. Legless always gave us a cheery smile as he shrugged deprecatingly at his tin as if asking pardon.

I made a point of going sorrowfully about the village lamenting the loss of my typewriter. I could, of course, buy a Spanish machine, but it would not serve me half as well.

The opinion of most people I spoke with was that the break-in had been done by *caminantes*; strange *gitanos* had been seen visiting houses in the *barrio gitano*.

A few days later, Isabel, our neighbourly fount of all knowledge, took me indoors. 'Alberto, *hijo*, my dear, go to Juli's house, she who has the son that is *lelo*, not all there. Perhaps . . .'

I thanked her and set off. Juli's house was in a tortuous *barrio* near the gypsy quarter. Juli herself greeted me courteously, but warily.

I came straight to the point. 'I hear you have my *máquina*.'

Without hesitation she nodded. '*Venga*, come,' she said. She led me into her backyard, pulled aside the tarpaulin in the corner, revealing my typewriter.

'*Mi hijo, señor*, as you know, my son is easily led. It was his companion, the *gitano* who lives – well you know where he lives – it was he, *maldita sea*, curse him, who led my poor son to go into your house and bring home the *máquina*. My son can neither read nor write, so what use is such a thing to him?'

I examined the typewriter; it appeared undamaged. I knew why she was so anxious. My suspicions were confirmed by the arrival of her sister, Lina, who now became spokesperson.

Lina was a woman in her early forties, but could have been at least ten years younger. She had already produced 13 children; from the look of her husband and herself, this was by no means the end of the saga.

'You know, *don* Alberto,' she began.

I could not help smiling. This was the first time she had honoured me with the title of '*don*'.

An intelligent woman, she knew perfectly well why I was smiling, and pitched in without preamble.

'My poor sister here' – she gestured as if to be sure I knew whom we were discussing – 'has no man. There has never been one, *qué vergüenza*, what a shame.'

She paused, as if expecting me to say something, then went on, her tone pleading.

'My sister's son, *el bastardo, qué vamos a hacer*, as you know is *bobo*, easily led. My sister also is' – she raised a finger to her forehead – 'and fears that you, *don* Alberto, not a native of this village, will send for the Guardia Civil. Then her poor Julio will go to prison. Then *qué vamos a hacer?*'

So this *was* why she was here. I waited long enough for her perturbation to grow; at least, I thought, both women deserved to suffer a little.

'*De nada*, it's nothing, Lina, do not worry. I have my *máquina*. I am content. This is a family thing. We do not want the Guardia Civil here in our village.'

Lina's attractive face lit up. '*Muchas gracias, don Alberto*,' she cried, '*mucha gracia*,' reverting in her relief to the local accent.

She turned to her sister, who perhaps had not understood my queer accent. 'See, Juli, see. Did I not tell you *elingléh es un buen hombre!*'

I'd had more than enough of this fulsome praise, not quite heartfelt, I suspected. I seized the typewriter. '*Hasta luego*,' I said as I picked my way down the treacherous path.

Only later did Isabel confide to us that nobody now could leave their doors open when *el bobo* was on the prowl. 'He slips through the door if your back is turned and steals any money lying about. Neighbours here in the *barrio* have lost money.'

Joan asked what they had done about it.

Isabel shrugged and looked at us in wonderment. 'What should they do? The poor mother has no control over Julio. The grandfather? He of the *nichos* does not care. All that Manolo cares about is doing little work, smoking, drinking, gossiping. We are all family here in the *pueblo*. No one would summon the Guardia Civil to settle a family matter.'

She glanced at me quizzically. 'And you, Alberto, what are you going to do?'

I answered her in the spirit in which she had asked the question. 'Nothing, Isabel. I have my *máquina*. That is all that matters.'

'Very wise, Alberto. There are some here who would wish you to get Julio put away. But . . . who knows who would then blame you, cease to regard Juanita and you as members of our family?'

I smiled. '*De acuerdo*, agreed, Isabel. *Muchas gracias*.'

One morning in town we saw this most attractive female (I speak for myself) coming towards us.

What a figure – medium height, ebony haired, two-hand-span waist gripped in a wide red belt with an elaborate white-metal buckle. Above, tight, tight in a black polo neck, two captivating breasts pouted most provocatively. Below, curving sharply outwards, magnificent haunches were equally tightly clad in black stretch pants that slid down over viewable thighs, calves, slim ankles. The patent shiny shoes were black, perilously high-heeled.

'You know who it is?' Joan said when the female was 20 yards from us.

'Should I?' I was slightly put out, as if her innocent question was not as innocent as it sounded. 'My eyes are not of the best.'

'Lina. Your typewriter, remember?'

'*Lina?* Surely not.'

'Yes, *Lina.* Here she comes. Speak to her.'

Joan need not have worried. Lina, mascared, rouged, powdered, lipsticked, looked (I thought) in her mid-twenties. She stopped in front of us.

'*Señora*,' she said, looking directly at Joan. 'How are you? And you, *don* Alberto, I find you well, I hope?'

I mumbled an appropriate answer. Joan said nothing.

Lina smiled, displaying model white teeth. '*Hasta luego, señores.* I have things to do.'

'I bet,' I muttered as I turned to feast my eyes on her as she swayed away tap-tapping.

'Did you get a good eyeful?' said Joan.

'I certainly did,' I replied with what dignity I could muster. '*Two* eyefuls.'

Back home, gossip that I am, I went next door to share my momentous news with neighbour Isabel. She waited calmly, knowing that something was up. I described Lina's appearance in some detail; no need at all to lay it on with a trowel.

'Did you know we have a *puta*, whore, in the village, Isabel? *Qué pueblo moderno tenemos*, what a modern village, we have.'

'Did you not already know of it, Alberto? The whole village knows. They say she earns plenty of *pasta*, cash.'

'But why is she doing this?'

'*Why?* It is a month now Lina left her man. Poor Carlos. Deserted, but *qué vamos a hacer? Dicen dicen*, they say, he decided –.' She hesitated. 'Well, Alberto, you had better ask the men if you want to know. I cannot tell you.'

Despite my urging, she did not say another word on the subject. She did, however, add Lina was now staying in the widow Ana's house, also in Calle Real near to her own. She sighed. 'Lina pays her well, I hear. It is a scandal. The whole village –.'

She broke off, and eyed me mischievously. 'No, that is not true. The women in our *barrio* are saying that certain men elsewhere in the village are now talking to Lina, where before they only greeted her in passing. Showing sympathy, they say, with her lonely state.'

'But I saw her the other day in the village shop. Dressed as she always dressed. No fancy –'

'*Claro*, of course. What need of such dress as you described here? The men here are not interested in dress, Alberto.' She smiled mischievously again at me, and I had a glimpse of the enchanting girl she must once have been. 'Not like you were in town, Alberto. And what does Juanita think?'

'She didn't say, Isabel, she didn't say.' I shook her playfully by the shoulder. Much appreciated; here we like to touch and be touched, an expression of true fond feeling.

I began to laugh. '*Las mujeres*, women!' I said. '*Hasta luego.*'

I made it my business to question one of my neighbours. He expressed surprise. '*Hombre*, what do you think?' He went through the motions of cutting with scissors. 'They say Carlos had had enough. So . . .' He knew there was no need for more words.

The gesture was one I was very familiar with. When I teased a young father who only had two or three children – 'Are you Spanish or English? Has your blood gone cold so soon?' – he invariably imitated scissors snipping, adding with a broad grin, '*Hombre, se ha cortado*, it has cut itself off.'

EPILOGUE

Our village is dying. Has been slowly for many years.

Sad, sad it is to see the unoccupied houses become ruins after their owners have died. The once flat pebbled roof gaping, the reeds collapsed, some fractured ones pointing skyward in protest.

Pause and gaze inside the thick earth-packed broken walls, areas of whitewash clinging yet. The *nicho* in which the Virgin reigned is still intact, but vacated. Above the gaping fireplace, askew but still in place, a coloured childlike picture of the Virgin nursing the child Jesus.

The fireplace itself, choked with a debris of fallen stones and earth and lime, still retains its structure. The great deeply striated log lintel stands guardian above it.

The shallow many-shelved cupboards let into the walls are doorless, although one brown shattered door hangs by a solitary hinge, resisting to the last. Nothing remains of the once-smooth concrete floor.

Sunt lacrimae rerum et mentem mortalia tangunt, There are tears shed for things and being mortal touches our heart.

Although comparatively few kilometres from the town, it was the villagers' culture, their whole age-old way of life, that kept them for so long literally untouched by time.

They knew they were, in the townsfolk's opinion, *una gente muy rara*, a most peculiar people, and they were proud of it.

Were they not all landowners? People of substance with their own houses? They were proud also that they had a thriving domestic economy, grew all they needed to live on, so only had to go to the town occasionally to buy things they could not produce.

They ate well. Unlimited fresh vegetables and fruit: what oranges, what bananas, tasted like theirs? And *carne*, meat? Sausages – *morcilla, butifarra, longaniza* (different kinds of sausage) – hams, bacon and salt pork from their own pigs, enough to last each family the whole year. Too much *grasa*, fat, they had heard, but *qué vamos a hacer*? Chickens and rabbits in plenty, eggs as well, and milk from the goats – everything.

They still believed that if a man would not work, neither should he eat. They honoured the saying of their forefathers: *Hay que trabajar*, We must work.

Everybody worked in the *vega*, parents and children. It was their duty, their way of life; they had no other interests; holidays were unheard of.

How fortunate they were, when in the town, so they heard, many were without work, even when they sought it.

La Iglesia de Nuestra Virgin de las Angustias, was the centre of their life, now as it had been since the thirteenth century. Religion was their secure base. The women and children went to mass on Sunday. The children, what with that and the *curas'* instruction, were all good Catholics. Communion was as important as births, weddings and funerals, a splendid *fiesta*.

The men? Well, the men went to mass only on special occasions; they were too busy in the fields, but this had always been the custom.

Our arrival in the village signalled the beginning of change. We were the first foreigners (or anyone else) that had ever lived here. Who, before we came, had even thought of a *cuarto de baño*? All, as I've said, soon had loos, indoor tap water and *duchas*, showers, often with bath, a radical departure from their traditional way of life. Instead of washing in a bucket, of squatting in the corral to add a little more dung, you could now have a shower or a bath, and sit at ease on the *aseo* – what a pleasure.

The coming of TV was the second and most important factor bringing change. The black-and-white sets, what looked like perpetual heavy rain falling, nevertheless gave them a window on the great world beyond.

175

Up to then they had been content to work the land as it had always been worked. Yet as time went on, things were getting worse. Often you had to jettison your crops, the prices were so low. Sometimes you could not sell a crop at any price.

They knew the reason of course, though were reluctant to admit it – the arrival of the new-fangled plastic houses elsewhere, curse them.

Colour TV arrived. Everyone, it seemed, had to have one. (They never understood why we had no telly.) Now they could view everything in glorious colour.

The grandparents regarded the telly as a welcome distraction. Their sons and their children saw it as a necessary part of their life, filling their leisure time. They could now receive the local programmes, and they became addicts.

The pressure on them to earn more to make their houses like those on the telly grew; houses with patterned padded armchairs and chairs; rugs, if not carpets, on the floor, so warm at night compared to their tiled floor; baths, not *duchas*; and fridges and everything.

But how to earn more to satisfy them and their clamorous children? Did they not already work from daylight to dark, seven days a week? As I've said, they knew the answer. At first reluctantly, then with ever-increasing enthusiasm, they acquired *invernaderos*, plastic houses. Huge ones like those other *agricultores* have. Then, like those elsewhere, they could export their produce. *Perfect* produce – you cannot export produce with insect damage and other blemishes, as now grown in the open fields.

They would join one of the big *cooperativos* that now existed farther away: they always paid a good price for perfect produce. The nearest cooperative was, though, too far away to take the crops by panniered mule. Besides, they would be producing far more than many mules could carry.

What, then? They must buy a *furgoneta*, a van – they had found out there were plenty of 'new second-hand' ones for sale. They could also use the van to take the family on *excursiones*, a new and exciting idea.

Invernaderos were very, very expensive; a big one would cost many thousands of pounds sterling. You had to hire one of the

176

specialist gangs of young men that went about the countryside doing this very hard and skilled work. That cost *un ojo y media*, an eye and a half. Then after three or four years, you had to renew the plastic; it rotted in this terrific heat. If you were unlucky and a violent storm came, then your plastic house could be blown away, then *qué vamos a hacer*?

Still, those with plastic houses were prospering, so why not them? They did not have the kind of money to pay for a plastic house to be erected, but the bank would lend them the money. *Ningun problema*, no problem; their land was their security. They would have to pay 15 to 17 per cent, but . . .

Mules and donkeys now became redundant and were sold off, except for a few that were kept for sentimental reasons by those about to give up working. The few little donkeys as well, alas.

The problem now was how to plough. Yes, if you were lucky you could find a pair of mules to hire from neighbours, but sometimes the fields had to be prepared and dunged ready for the next crop and it was not always convenient to hire the mules.

This problem was solved by two enterprising landless lads purchasing rotavators small enough to get into the corners where the mules could get, and along the edges of the irregularly shaped *parcelas*.

Our neighbour, Juan White Mule, kept his mule. '*Hombre*, their *máquinas* drink *gasolina*. What expense. They do not dung the soil and they ruin the make-up of the soil. Neither, in my opinion, do they plough like our old ploughs, like mine still does. But, *qué vamos a hacer*? Necessary progress, so they say, they and their *invernaderos*. I am glad I am too old for such nonsense. Remember my words, Alberto. It will not be long before we have many new *agricultores here* – the banks.'

The older people lamented the coming of the plastic, the noise of the vans and the rotavators, and the accompanying changes as much as we did. But they accepted it in their usual fatalistic way. So did we. Soon the signs of increasing prosperity began to manifest themselves, and we were glad. All their hard work was now at last being adequately rewarded.

* * *

The village school was an all-age one. Attendance was very irregular; much depended on what work had to be done in the fields. Two rooms, two teachers, there was always bedlam when we passed.

A scandal occurred when the man teacher was abruptly dismissed – no one in the village would tell us why. I asked Fausto. He averred that Sebastián had merely shown his affection a little too strongly to one child, for he and his poor wife were childless. I was none the wiser; Joan was slightly put out that I had not done a better job of quizzing Fausto.

Soon after the coming of the plastic, the seniors were bussed to the secondary school in the town.

What a momentous change. Now they witnessed in actuality some of the things they had only previously vicariously experienced on TV. What ways. What language. Another world, this world of the town. Much impressed, the seniors brought home these ways and that language, used expressly to impress the younger children and their parents.

Soon after the seniors had changed schools, the roof of what was now the primary school fell in, luckily at night, during a violent rainstorm. Paco was long since dead, his bakehouse empty. Temporary school was set up in the bakehouse. The first week in February was rainy – most unusual here, where there is no measurable rainfall. Consequently, no one has a raincoat; all have umbrellas for the occasional light shower.

As we passed the open bakehouse door one day during that rainy week, we saw a host of open umbrellas under which the children were sheltering, doing the best they could with their free hand, the roof being as leaky as a basket. Never loath to seize their moment, they greeted us ecstatically and invited us in, their little voices raised in warm welcome. The two women teachers did not seem pleased. The children had all used our names – were we not *familia*? – and we *were* very pleased.

Increasing prosperity, closely linked to the use of *invernaderos*, led to the establishment of new *conurbaciones*, miniature towns, and additions to those already existing. Their principal feature was the large number of duplexes, first houses, for the increasingly moneyed young *agricultores* and their growing families.

What more natural than that our village's engaged couples, fed on the telly, should wish to go and live in a new duplex with all modern conveniences: what an enticing prospect. Far more life there as well, with modern shops, a supermarket, discos and dances and clubs and . . .

And very important, they would be living only a few kilometres from their parents, so they could still bundle the children into the van and dump then on the *abuelos*, grandparents, whenever they wished.

Nor were the fiancés now prepared for the girl to wait until her father was pleased to release her. They would marry when *they* decided. If the father blocked the way, then the girl, as I've said, would get a bun in the oven. The rush to church would be precipitate, groom and bride radiating joy and satisfaction.

Can you wonder, then, that the village *is* slowly dying? Yes, there are still some young families living here, and we have the pleasure of seeing and talking with the children.

We know three families in which the couples are wedded to their own parents and the old way of life. They live next door to their parents, and seemingly rely on their support. Besides, how much cheaper it is to live well here. With their vans (one family even has a car, the gift of their parents) they can quickly go into town or wherever they wish.

The other few young families are simply waiting until they have accumulated enough money to put down a deposit on a duplex and furnish it.

We feel this leaking away of life very keenly. Soon, too, we shall probably move. We look back on our life here with no regrets. We know how fortunate we were to have, through sheer serendipity, found our enchanted house and to have lived here for so long when this village was quite literally untouched by time.

Elegy for a Village

Oranges fall unheeded,
Relight their yellow lamps
That brighten as day dies.

The old man ploughing
Near the orange trees
Stops the sweating mules,
Wipes the sweat from his face.

He picks up an orange,
Monkey-tails the skin,
Sucks the sweet, sweet flesh,
The day's work done at last.

Across the river, a tractor
In triumph celebrates
The end of the old man's world.

Yet meet we shall, and part, and meet again,
Where dead men meet on lips of living men.

Samuel Butler, *Life After Death*